A KNIGHT IN
SHINING ARMOR

Also by Harvey A. Hornstein:

Social Intervention: A Behavioral Science Approach with W. W. Burke, B. A. Bunker, M. Gindes, R. Lewicki (1971)
The Social Technology of Organization Development with W. W. Burke (1972)
Applying Social Psychology with M. Deutsch (1975)
Cruelty and Kindness: A New Look at Aggression and Altruism (1976)
Managing Human Forces in Organizations with Madeline Heilman (1982)
Managerial Courage: Revitalizing Your Company Without Sacrificing Your Job (1986)

A KNIGHT IN SHINING ARMOR

Understanding Men's Romantic Illusions

HARVEY A. HORNSTEIN, Ph.D.

WILLIAM MORROW AND COMPANY, INC.
New York

1500

Library of Congress Cataloging-in-Publication Data

Hornstein, Harvey A., 1938–
    A knight in shining armor: understanding men's romantic illusions / by Harvey Hornstein
        p.   cm.
    Includes bibliographical references.
    ISBN 0-688-09843-6
    1. Masculinity (Psychology) 2. Men—Psychology. 3. Sex role.
I. Title.
BF692.5.H66   1991
155.3'32—dc20

                                                                91-9321
                                                                CIP

Printed in the United States of America

First Edition

1 2 3 4 5 6 7 8 9 10

BOOK DESIGN BY RICHARD ORIOLO

155.332
H 78
c.1

For Madeline
and our daughters,
Jessica, Alison, and Erica

ACKNOWLEDGMENTS

I was able to write this book because of the cooperation and courage of 150 men and women, who spent more than four hundred hours answering my questions about their romantic relationships.

Their stories revealed how these relationships were regularly disrupted by men's excessive expectations of themselves and of women. I learned about both traditional men and seemingly enlightened ones trying to perform modern equivalents of Prince Charming feats, expecting that they were required if women were going to provide them with happily forever afters. Emotion-filled accounts of love affairs, marriages, and divorces described the pressure experienced by men as well as the rage and oppression inflicted by them on women who, in their eyes, "failed" to produce an undisturbed, happily forever after. The telling took courage. The memories were both happy and sad. They laughed and cried. So did I. For contributing their time, and for sharing precious parts of their lives with me (and with you), I thank them.

Gerry McCauley and Maria Guarnaschelli offered their commitment and support before there was a final product, this book. Their faith encouraged me, and I am grateful to both of them. I also want to thank Maria for her insightful editorial input. It helped enormously.

Madeline Heilman has been my partner in creating what

I now know is the closest thing that real, nonfairy–tale folks can have to happily forever after. She is a successful co-professional whose ideas challenged me to improve every page of this book. She is also mother to our daughters, Alison and Erica, and stepmother to my eldest daughter, Jessica.

Through the years that we have been together, Madeline has helped me to learn that happily forever after is sometimes an untidy place where, in fact, people are not always entirely happy. With gratitude and love, I am dedicating this book to Madeline, and also to our daughters. My prayer is that their experience with us as a couple, as well as this book's contents, help them to better manage the real-life temptations symbolized by the myth of Prince Charming.

CONTENTS

10

CONTENTS

PRINCE CHARMING'S PLIGHT

. . . *September 4, 1989*—Labor Day. I met Amy last night. My hopes are soaring. Very special things seem possible. Caution—don't let it run away with you. But it does seem as if, finally, there's someone who can give me what I want and need. She's cheerful, lovely. . . . We talked for hours. I went on for too long about jazz, but it really seemed as if she wanted to learn. It made me feel so good. We're set for dinner on Thursday. I've got butterflies. Postsummer resolution: more exercise.

. . . *September 5, 1989*—It's A.M. and I'm rushing to leave for work. I'm nervous. It's "the doubts" again. I had a dream last night—

I'm in the water. There's been an accident—a sinking. A lifeboat comes by and I climb in. Other men are there. A lifeboat filled with women drifts alongside. They need help because none are able to row. How can we row for the two boats, which suddenly seem huge? The sides are high—too high, for normal. I am forced to row with my hands and arms raised as if to say, "I surrender." My arms feel limp, watery. My hands and fingers aren't able to close firmly. They lack strength. I don't feel the water's resistance against my oars. I'm not accomplishing anything.

At some point we tell the women to get down, as if that will lighten the load of their boat. Somehow we get to shore. I'm out of the boat, standing on the side, smiling—waiting for something. What? The women walk by. None say anything. I get very upset. My face feels hot. I am angry, and start shouting at them.

Asleep, I know it's a nightmare and I want to wake up.

. . . *March 27, 1990*—I'm going to end it with Amy, finally. No more back and forth. I don't see any future. Amy doesn't agree, although she's ambivalent. When we argue it's, "You don't take me seriously. You don't even know me." Is it true? I don't see it. What more does she want? And what about what I want?

I still believe that with the right woman, special things happen. Question: Will there be one for me?

Has it occurred to you that Prince Charming had problems too? It never occurred to this diary's author. Like thousands of other men, he suffered man-servant syndrome. His relationships with women were contaminated with its emotional poison.

Gregory Kaiser* is another victim of man-servant syn-

---

* In order to protect the identities of the people I interviewed, all the names used throughout this book are fictitious.

drome. Who is Gregory Kaiser? How shall I answer? "Just another Joe. No one very special." Gregory is half-owner of a retail shop dealing in foreign-auto parts. He's five feet ten or eleven, fit and well groomed, with a broad smile and a firm handshake. His ruddiness speaks to you of time spent outdoors, and his hands communicate manual labor.

Who is Gregory Kaiser? One of 150 men and women whom I studied in order to learn about man-servant syndrome. His time with me happened to be two weeks, to the day, after his forty-first birthday, twelve years after he married Evelyn—his first and only wife—and eight years after his only child, Edward, was born.

Who is Gregory Kaiser? He is a victim of man-servant syndrome. Seeking fulfillment as a man through his relationships with women, he finds only frustration. He is indentured to women, but craves independence. He controls them and imagines that he is being caring. Gregory Kaiser's own words are eloquent in their portrayal of the syndrome and the costs that it exacts from him as well as so many other unsuspecting men and women. Here is part of what he told me:

Being in a relationship with a woman is important to me. I've always sought it out. There's a kind of emotional prosperity—a kind of fullness—at least in the beginning.

(My ears perked up at the qualifying "in the beginning," and I asked what he meant by that.)

In the beginning? Well, I suppose it's common enough for men. You know, in the beginning you expect great things. There is excitement, promise, then . . . something dies. Not exactly dies, but I always have a sense that something essential, at the center, is missing. Something that should be there. There should be more. I don't feel right. What I give and what I get is kind of out of whack. . . .

You know, it's funny that we're having this conversation because it's something that I've thought a lot about lately. (I've grown accustomed to hearing all sorts of men say this to me: white, Hispanic, and black, gay and straight, twenty-year-olds and seventy-year-olds. Lots of men, it seems, spend lots of time thinking about what's missing in their relationships with women. I said none of this to Gregory Kaiser. He continued speaking.)

My marriage is O.K., but I've been needing my own space for a while. It's like, I've done what I can, now it's my time. I don't make it obvious or anything, but I need a little more for me. I'm not saying that I'm going to leave or anything, but . . . in my own head, I've kind of pulled back. It's just damned hard to keep delivering!

I think that's it. Demands. Women push. Maybe not in so many words, but you can feel it. It's not enough. I try to do right, really work my butt off, help—you know, be attentive. Take care of stuff. Say, "How are you?" "You look great." Women respond to that. Not that I do it for that reason, but there should be something for me. I mean, I need something too. Now you're going to ask me what that something is.

(I nodded both to affirm his insight and encourage him to tell me that "something". He understood the signal and went on.)

You know how sometimes women make you feel—like a Prince Charming. Now I feel . . . I don't know . . . not like a Prince Charming—sort of like—well, something else. . . . I guess I'd like that something that lets me feel like a Prince Charming again. I also guess that I still haven't told you what that something is.

*   *   *

He hadn't, but that was O.K. After studying 149 other men and women I now know what that "something" is. It is the core of an impossible-to-fulfill fantasy that all men have at some point in their lives and that possesses some for their whole life. It is a fantasy that fuels men's passions for women as well as their need to dominate them. Most tragically, it is a fantasy that destroys men's relationships with women, causing the men to feel betrayed. A deal was broken. A bounty, which was promised, earned, and owed, was not delivered.

There is a bit of Gregory Kaiser in all men. All men have had similar thoughts and feelings. But not all men remain victims of man-servant syndrome. Some learn to avoid the syndrome's worst costs. Their lives are not punctuated by relationships with women that roller-coaster through service-anger cycles of increasing intensity until some psychological or actual physical breakup occurs. These men do not feel restricted, stifled, and oppressed in their relationships with women. Nor are they oppressors of women.

How do some men avoid these costs? By lots of self-awareness and hard work on themselves to achieve insight into the syndrome, often carried out hand in hand with a woman who shares the insight.

Gregory Kaiser's words contained no evidence that he was loosening himself from the syndrome's grip. Nonetheless, what he said may be useful to the rest of us who want to learn what man-servant syndrome is all about.

A Play in Three Acts

When men are in the throes of man-servant syndrome, their relationships with women are like a three-act play. Each act has key lines, spoken by Man-Servant, that tell what the act is all about:

Act One: Wanting and Serving

At first I felt like I couldn't be without her. Then, later, there was less joy. The electricity was gone. It became stifling, sometimes painfully so. I felt less good about myself, my life. I craved something more. I convinced myself that if I worked still harder to make her happy, it would be O.K. She'd come through. I'd be a somebody. It would be special, magic.

Act Two: Disillusionment and Blame

I'm not perfect, but I did my best. Made every reasonable effort. But it was never enough. I feel that she could have done more. Made it different. It never happened.

Act Three: Rage and Oppression

I've had it. At some point a man must stand up and say, "Enough." It's my life too. I know that there's got to be something more out there.

The play is a tragedy. Flaws in the principle character, Man-Servant, guarantee his downfall. Possessed by a self-defeating view of male-female relationships, Man-Servant is tempted into a quest without end: Prove himself worthy and women will give him their bounty, affirming that he's a real man.

It's all smoke and mirrors, an illusion. Man-Servant is working hard to show that he should receive a bounty that no woman is able to give. His efforts are Sisyphean. His only reward will be endless cycles of relationships with women that begin with wanting and serving, and finish in rage and oppression.

Gregory Kaiser's views were those of a person suffering man-servant syndrome. He experienced his relationships with women as unbalanced.

Statements by Man-Servants: Some Telltale Signs of the Syndrome

Women have ways of getting what they want out of a man.

A man will naturally tend toward overoptimism in the beginning of his relationship with a woman.

Women show gratitude when it buys them something.

No matter what a man does a woman will bargain for still more.

A man gives and gives without getting back from a woman what he deserves.

Women have ways of making a man wonder whether they'll ever be satisfied.

If a woman really made the effort a man could feel really special.

Women are masters at pretending to be less powerful than they really are.

Despite appearances men are often controlled by women.

Women conveniently seem to forget the promises that they make.

A woman will often complain about the things a man does without admitting that he's doing them for her.

Like other man-servants, Gregory Kaiser felt that he was giving to women, but not getting back that "something" he wanted in return. He knew pitifully little about that "something" except that it would let him "feel like Prince Charming." What of Prince Charming? Who is he really, and what did he do?

Prince Charming Is Something Else

Prince Charming is a fairy-tale character, but he can't be written off as simply make-believe. Fairy tales are more than meaningless fiction. They are to a society what furniture is to a well-designed room: It blends in, both reflecting and supporting the motif of the room. Fairy tales, too, express, reflect, and support society's motif in the advice that they give about fundamental human concerns: the importance and meaning of truth, beauty, courage, cowardice, greed, envy, loyalty, and love. Through their characters' strengths, weaknesses, virtues, misdeeds, cleverness, errors, successes, and failures, fairy tales communicate a social consensus about the management of these universal concerns.

The tongue-in-cheek exaggeration that follows illustrates the one important message communicated by the Prince Charming-rescuer stories:

Dear Brother Grimm,

I'm unattached and have been told that the fairest virgin in the land is locked away in a keep some distance from my castle. The way is dangerous. Dragons, swamps, and who knows what threaten anyone who approaches the place where she is imprisoned. It is said that she will join the man who rescues her and his life will be happy ever after. What shall I do?

Dear Castle Owner,
Go after it! Show that you've got the stuff. Be persistent,
decisive, wise, brave, and powerful. You've got the castle, now
rescue the fair maiden and she'll make you feel like a real prince.

Prince Charming–type characters occur in a number of man-rescues-woman fairy tales, as in Western literature's popular "Sleeping Beauty," "Snow White," and "Cinderella." The typical interpretation of these stories has been from the heroine's perspective. I've no quarrel with this interpretation, only regret. The heroine's perspective is but one half of the story. It shortchanges men by neglecting Prince Charming's plight and its implications for understanding man-servant syndrome. Interpretations from the heroine's perspective find these fairy tales delivering a message that simultaneously reflects and supports society's stereotype of women: If you want your Prince Charming, don't be too assertive, daring, intelligent, accomplished, or decisive. The list goes on, but it can easily be summarized by "Woman, don't show any of the qualities that society values in a man. Helplessness, passivity, and dependency are what you want. Be a sleeping beauty, flawless and virginal, like unsullied white snow. Have the domestic talent of a scullery maid, and someday your prince will come. He'll lift you in rapture to a castle in the clouds. There you will dwell, adored, protected, and provided for, like a princess, happily ever after."

This doesn't happen. If a woman doesn't feel like a princess, then, aside from temporary relief, there's nothing a man can do to change it. Men cannot perform the fabled magic of a Prince Charming, producing an undisturbed, halcyon forever after. Women who vainly hope for a Prince

Charming are possessed by the female counterpart to man-servant syndrome. The awful consequence of this is evident in a confession made by Colette Dowling, the author of a best-selling book, *The Cinderella Complex:* "I felt strong and effective precisely because I was acting on behalf of my husband, my own image protected, my personal talents untried. I would have made a top-notch executive secretary, cutting through swathes of red tape . . . seeing to it that the other guy—my boss, my protector—always got what he wanted [pp. 138–139]."

Dowling's experiences and those of other women who suffer the female counterpart to the man-servant syndrome are awful. But equally awful is the way this counterpart becomes a bit of the fertilizer that nourishes men's acquisition of the syndrome itself. Men, you see, are daily pressured to live up to the stereotypical image of boss, protector, and all-around performer of Prince Charming–like feats.

Ultra-Man

Prince Charming and other male-rescuers are not your everyday Joes. These men kill, outwit, imprison, and otherwise immobilize fantastic adversaries. They defeat witches, ogres, ogresses, sorcerers (the evil kind), and various monsters. Oceans, dark woods, deserts, mountains, valleys, pits, raging rivers, caves, and caverns are mastered by these heroes. For example, Prince Charming, Sleeping Beauty's rescuer, demonstrates his magic and machismo when, in order to reach Beauty, he risks crossing a wall of thorns that had already taken the lives of several previous suitors. For him, these deadly thorns turn into a wall of lovely and penetrable flowers (an obvious symbol for the virginal deflowering that he will soon enjoy). Why should the wall be so transformed? Presumably because his "manly" efforts, persistence, and patience earned him the maiden's bounty.

Snow White's rescuers (there are several) are not lesser men. Her first rescuer is a hunter who defies Snow White's evil stepmother by releasing rather than killing the maiden. Hunters are popular male-rescuers. Little Red Riding Hood's rescuer, you will remember, was also a hunter. Hunting is a quintessentially masculine occupation. Hunters provide and protect. They have weapons and skills that give them power to take life (in contrast to a woman's power to give life).

Snow White is next rescued by a group of workaholic dwarfs, little men who forego any fun and recreation (until Snow White's arrival) in order to do their work as miners. It's obviously no accident that they're miners. Mining, like hunting, is stereotypically masculine work. It's a dangerous pursuit that requires the alteration of a hostile, resistant environment in order to extract the valuables that it possesses. Mines are fertile places for accumulating proof that you're a *man*.

Snow White's final male-rescuer is a prince. Brave, persistent, and adventurous, he travels some distance to reach her. Then, he negotiates with the obstinate and potentially dangerous dwarfs, offering them anything that they want in exchange for Snow White, whose image of perfection testifies to the bounty that she possesses. Evidently, in addition to his other masculine qualities, this Prince Charming is also capable of magic, since his kiss undoes the evil stepmother's poison-induced coma.

As I said, Prince Charming and the other male-rescuers

are not your everyday Joes. They are ultra-men who tend toward being exceptional in wealth, strength, and daring. These extraordinary fellows are often intelligent and uncommonly persistent in their dedication to an effort. The ones who get romantically involved with the stories' heroines are flawlessly handsome men, who are also capable of acting on the world in ways that promise to transform the heroines' lives into happy forever afters. But just as the fairy-tale heroines display what women should bring to male-female relationships if they are to be successful, the male-rescuers' qualities reflect and support society's stereotypes of what men must bring to male-female relationships if they, too, are to be successful. These stereotypes are the requisite male competency cluster.

The Male Competency Cluster

Modern social science tells us that the personal qualities male-rescuers demonstrate when they slay dragons and overcome other supernatural challenges are being demanded of today's men. This is one reason for the continuing popularity of fairy tales. Their message has a home.

About a decade ago, in a research study, men and women were presented with a picture of other men and women gathered in a group. When asked, "Who's the leader?" in the picture, both men and women tended to answer that the person in charge was one of the men.

This is a single finding, from a single study, but it reflects the results of scores of other investigations in a wide variety of situations, with a wide variety of respondents: Men and women choose men, rather than women, as competent, take-charge people.

Interpretations of these findings have placed emphasis on how tendencies to see men as belonging in positions of power result in discrimination toward women. It's true that this happens, but the negative consequences for men, which is the story's other half, should not be ignored. The same social forces that bias the perception and treatment of women, place pressure on men to be *leaders,* to take charge and be competently in control.

In the picture, a woman wasn't identified as leading the group because that role doesn't fit the sex-role stereotype of women. Research evidence continues to show that today's women are expected to be like many familiar fairy-tale heroines: gentle, tactful, neat, quiet, emotionally sensitive, and capable of expressing tender feelings. Their domain is the internal world of emotion. From it, supposedly, comes a bounty of nurturance, compassion, cooperativeness, affection, empathy, sensuousness, and sensitivity. Women's bounty is libidinal. They are supposed to possess the competency to make others feel good about themselves and their relationships.

Men, by contrast, are stereotyped as independent, objective, logical, active, dominant, forceful, and competitive. Like their fairy-tale counterparts, men are expected to be leaders and champions—ambitious, decisive, adventurous, and self-confident. Their domain is the external world, where they shape and change things. If women's bounty is libidinal, the men's is material. What men are supposed to bring to relationships is an unfailing competency to successfully challenge and alter the environment so as to provide, protect, and, if need be, rescue.

Of course, these sex-role stereotypes are not accurate reflections of how men and women really are. They are idealized, culturally biased prescriptions for how men and women should be. Subtly inserted into people's lives, hidden from conscious thought, they tickle each sex's fancy with vague promises of the bounty that the other sex is capable of providing. It's what keeps the would-be Prince Charmings of the world going: The maiden's deathlike existence, coldness, and unavailability are magically undone when a man's feats establish him as a bona fide, worthy possessor of the male competency cluster's material bounty. Then the maiden becomes warm and available, offering him her bounty, which will transform his emotional world just as he is transforming her material one. He will achieve Gregory Kaiser's dream and feel like a prince.

MAN-SERVANT SYNDROME

Everyman's problem is that the male competency cluster is an impossible dream. Like some unreachable, exploding supernova, its brightness shines in sharp contrast with the successes that men actually achieve. Its perfection makes a man's errors, hesitations, and cautions seem ugly. Inevitably men experience a gap between what is and what they imagine ought to be. The gap fills them with doubt and self-blame, further undermining the self-assurance and confidence *men* are supposed to possess. As effect becomes cause, the gap widens, creating still more doubt and self-blame. A deadly cycle is engaged. It's like a tragedy in three acts (*wanting and serving, disillusionment and blame, rage and oppression*), in which the male protagonist, Man-Servant, plays like a prince but feels like a frog, gawky and repulsive.

Wanting and Serving

If the fairy tales of "Sleeping Beauty," "Snow White," and
"Cinderella" capture the social psychological mechanics of
women's disempowerment and self-denigration, then
"Beauty and the Beast" and "The Frog Prince" capture the
mechanics that turn men into man-servants.

Kiss me, I'm a frog. "Beauty and the Beast" and "The
Frog Prince" belong to a class of fairy tales known as the
animal-groom (as in bridegroom) stories. Their pattern is
simple: Man, in the form of a repulsive animal, wants
(really needs) a female. He serves her, expecting his due
in return. What he gets are broken promises. Women in
these stories are fickle, even perfidious, and certainly not
to be trusted. Undaunted, the creature persists in his service and adoration. Finally, the maiden yields (usually because her father, an obvious representation of all male
authority, intervenes and instructs her to behave herself)
and through her love (commonly symbolized by a kiss or
a night in bed), the repulsive creature is transformed into
a prince of a man.

What do these stories tell readers about male-female relationships? A great deal, although most interpretations of
the animal-groom stories neglect their implications for understanding man-servant syndrome. Indeed, some also actually manifest the syndrome's symptoms by implying that
men are O.K., but women need to remedy their sexually
dysfunctional attitudes so that they can share their bounty.
These stories, the thesis goes, "convey that it is mainly the
female who needs to change her attitude about sex from
rejecting it to embracing it, because as long as sex appears

to her ugly and animal-like, it remains animalistic in the male. . . . As long as one partner loathes sex, the other cannot enjoy it; as long as one partner views it as animal-like, the other remains partially an animal to himself and his partner."

From the perspective of man-servant syndrome, this interpretation is self-serving. It states that women are to blame when men experience themselves as repulsive. Furthermore, this interpretation gives men a splendid excuse for acting as man-servants. They can serve women by rescuing them from their afflictions. Once rescued, like Sleeping Beauty, Snow White, and Cinderella, the now healthy females will be grateful, able, and willing to deliver their bounty to the deserving male-rescuers. How perfect, and how wrong!

In my view, this interpretation is propaganda. It tries to provide intellectual justification for the behavior of men affected by man-servant syndrome, but actually misses entirely the message communicated by the animal-groom stories. "Men," these stories advise, "women have the power to take away what ails you. Then can turn you into a prince of a man. All you need to do is serve them as a man should, by providing, protecting, and adoring." From this perspective, intimacy is an exchange of giving and receiving. Women give their bounty to men in return for what they have received from them.

Instrumental intimacy. Man-servant syndrome rounds out an insidious reciprocal dependency between the sexes. Men and women behave in ways that they hope will ensure delivery of the other sex's bounty. What each sex hopes the other will deliver differs, as do their ways of getting it.

What both have in common, however, is the futility of their quest.

Women are suckered into awaiting a Prince Charming who will provide, protect, and adore them. In exchange for that dream, which is never to be fulfilled, a woman becomes a man's passive appendage, acting on his behalf, never threatening his status, which the two collude in pretending is superior.

Men, on the other hand, are conned into seeking a female response that will make them feel powerful and potent, affirming their manhood finally and completely, removing any hint of "frogness." In exchange for that never-to-be-fulfilled dream, men provide, protect, and adore women.

This vacuous imitation of intimacy has dreadful consequences. Love, affection, and respect are not emotions that man-servants truly feel. One man I interviewed offered a sad insight: "I never understood that women gave gifts. All I thought they were capable of was extending gratitude."

It's a wonderful distinction: gifts as opposed to gratitude. Women give in exchange for a man's effort, which is advance payment for the joys that a man imagines a woman can provide. For men afflicted by the syndrome, there is no loving gift, given freely, not owed or offered in exchange for anything. These men always feel "on duty." Their every act is potentially an offering, to be presented at a maiden's altar in the vain hope that she will find it sufficient and yield in return what she possesses. Their every deed, therefore, must be worthy. To make it seem so, these men advertise themselves, often falsely.

Male advertisements. As with so many areas in life where less availability means greater value, the more a man doubts that he has the male-competency-cluster attributes that merit a woman's bounty, the more precious the bounty appears, the more he wants it and the more he wants others—especially women—to believe that he has the stuff it takes to deserve it. It's the only way to make his inner world right, sweeping away doubts and psychological blemishes.

Now the deception begins. A man pretends to possess the very characteristics that he doubts he has in order to secure the woman's bounty. It doesn't work. No woman can perform the magic that he wants. (Although many women, trying vainly to live up to their stereotype as possessors of the libidinal bounty, get seduced into trying to turn discontented frogs into blissful princes.) In the end, our hero still feels gawky and repulsive, or as Gregory Kaiser said, "not like a Prince Charming." If he is unable to understand that the disappointment is a product of setting impossible-to-attain standards for himself combined with impossible-to-attain expectations of women, then his need for deception, including self-deception, and boasting grows as the failure to win the bounty adds fresh doubts to his already tarnished self-image.

The evidence is there for anyone to see. Compared to women, men are less open to negative feedback. They tend to be more close-mouthed about their inner experiences and defensive when they feel that their self-esteem is being threatened. And, if one compares objective indicators of ability with the estimates that men and women make of their future success, one thing emerges clearly: Men overestimate, and women underestimate, performance. Why? Because neither sex can win the other's bounty unless he or she shows the requisite competency cluster.

Ironies of a man-servant. The observations illustrate the different but equally tragic burdens that society places on men and women. In order to pretend that they possess the requisite competency cluster, women are pressured into self-diminishing self-presentation and men into boastful self-presentation.

There are three ironic and psychologically catastrophic consequences for men afflicted by man-servant syndrome. First, *men's pursuit of excessively high standards nearly guarantees that they will end up feeling like failures.* When this happens, their discontent with themselves and their "what makes Sammy run" approach to life often puzzles onlookers, who wonder why people so seemingly successful should behave as if they were failing. The problem is that, in their own eyes, these men feel they *are* failing. What we have here is a tyranny of achievement, the male counterpart to women's tyranny of nonachievement.

The second irony is that *although man-servants are motivated by the fantastic belief that achievement of bliss rests upon a woman's affirmation of them, they are destined never to feel fully satisfied by what a woman does for them.*

There are two reasons for this. First, women cannot perform the extraordinary transformational magic that man-servants fantasize they can. And second, apropos of the gift-gratitude distinction, man-servants are fated to be disappointed because, in their instrumental interpretation of experience, women give to men only in gratitude for what they get from men. Therefore, women's giving can never be experienced as an affirmation of who the men are as people, but only as the repayment of what men have done for them. If men want more of a woman's giving, then they had better remain "on duty."

The third and final irony for men experiencing the syndrome is implied by the first two: *Although giving to women is man-servants' raison d'être, they will never feel that they have given what is required to satisfy women.* Two causes combine to produce this irony. First, the standards that lure man-servants are always excessive, vague, and therefore unreachable. Thus, whatever they give feels unsatisfactory to them. The second cause is that the fantastic, magical affirmation of manhood these men require from women is beyond mortal women's capabilities to give. Consequently, man-servants' work is never done and, once again, they are compelled to remain "on duty."

The effects of these ironies pervade man-servants' lives with women, but they are starkly evident in their sexual experiences.

One forty-seven-year-old physician told me, "I'm not a lover. I'm an observer, not a participant in sex."

I inquired about his sense of what his wife's experiences were when they made love.

"She gets turned on," he said, "and reaches climax almost always. Not always through intercourse, but manually or whatever. But," he explained, and here's the key, "for that to happen I feel I've got to be like an orchestra conductor. You know [now he waved his arms about], carefully signaling, keeping time . . . a real virtuoso. So . . . I suppose that the best way to describe it is that I'm watching to make sure that she's satisfied. Then, no matter what she does or how she responds, I don't feel really involved, lost in it, spontaneous. Maybe no one does. Who knows? It's kind of . . . I've got to take care of her so that . . . I can have my experience. So that it can happen. But when it happens, it's sort of too distant, apart, and I'm not sure it's different for her. It's funny."

A twenty-year-old aspiring artist cleverly called it "sexual stage management," but it's not at all funny. These two men and many others whom I interviewed are engaging in something akin to a religious sex ritual.

Throughout history there are examples of ritual sex being used as a means of worshiping female deities. Since humans were unable to fathom the mystery of fertility (that is, the bringing forth of life), sexual acts were performed as part of a prescribed ritual in order to entreat the female deity to release her life-sustaining bounty. Man-servants also perform, sexually and in other ways, hoping that, because of their efforts, they will be granted a woman's life-giving bounty. When it doesn't happen, man-servants become disillusioned and lay the blame on women.

Disillusionment and Blame

My friends said, "You've got it all, house, cars, lovely wife, kids, everything." Objectively, I suppose they were right, but it didn't feel that way, I can tell you. I was miserable inside. A long time passed before I let that out to Sandy {his wife}.

Joe Handle-Everything, that's what I was supposed to be. I'd slave away to get it all.

("Who did you slave for?" I asked Daniel Edenlost, a thirty-three-year-old stockbroker who was in the midst of a divorce.)

Who for? For her—the family. I mean, I was a slave—but not for me. If they were happy then I could be. I mean that. It sounds mushy but I mean it.

("Were they happy?" I asked, already sensing what the answer would be.)

Who knows? I know that I wasn't. When could I let it out? I was feeling miserable, but I had responsibility. But somehow none of it mattered. She said—Sandy—"It was good." She felt that I'd done well. She was puzzled—tried to reassure me. Others— friends—did too. But that always made me angry with her. It made it worse that she said, "You're great. . . . It's O.K. . . . Let up." I knew that she didn't understand and couldn't give me what I wanted, but I didn't tell her for a long while.

(I pressed him a bit. "What was it you wanted?")

Well—an alternative—another way to be—enough sacrifice without return.

(At the risk of being seen as an ally of his wife, I said, "I'm confused, wasn't that what she was saying? 'Let up— it's O.K.'?")

Well, maybe, but it didn't feel that way. To me, the bottom line is that she didn't have a clue about what was happening to me or what I needed. I needed to grow, be different—to me, she wanted more of the same—"It's O.K." That's what "it's O.K." means. It was bullshit—excuse the French—it wasn't O.K. I felt like hell every day. I needed to be my own man and was getting nothing from her.

Women are man-servants' enemies. It is the price they pay for being seen as rulers of man's access to sexual salvation.

Trapped by the three ironies, and still trying to be superior, man-servants displace their disappointment and frustration onto women. "I gave and gave," says Man-Servant. "Did my best. But mostly what I felt from her were demands for still more. It's exhausting. She's blocking my path to better things."

In literature women like this are called "shrews." Shrews demand things, but offer no promise of a libidinal bounty. I have no doubt that some women actually qualify as shrews, but insofar as the relationship between man-servants and shrews is concerned, it seems likely that the shrew these men experience is largely in the eye and ear of the man-servant beholder. The most fundamental demands that he hears, and then attributes to *her,* come from within him. Some accusations of failure may originate with her, but they also come loudly from within him. He is the one who is unable to accept and experience whatever affirmation she offers. She may have doubts about his competencies and successes, but he has his own very profound and morbid doubts. She may be a shrew, but a worse one dwells within him. For him, it's just more comfortable to see the shrew-ishness as being part of her, out there. Then there's someone to blame and sometimes beat up.

One study of wife beaters, in fact, actually reports that the men involved perceived the women they brutalized as shrewlike. They described the women as sexually frigid (giving no bounty), as well as aggressive, efficient, and masculine. (What can a man do for a woman who already has the material bounty that a man is supposed to deliver?) Whether the women involved were actually these things is irrelevant. The point is that man-servants' inevitable disillusionment causes them to see women this way, and then, in turn, the relationship with these imagined shrews further peaks man-servants' frustration and rage. There's nothing that a man can give them, since they've already usurped the male competency cluster by being aggressive, efficient, and masculine.

The fair maidens in "Beauty and the Beast" and "The Frog Prince" also have attributes capable of causing a man's disillusionment. They are fickle and perfidious, promising to come across with their bounty if the creature serves them and then reneging on the promise. In the end, only the firm exercise of male authority makes the bounty available.

The same pattern is characteristic of men experiencing man-servant syndrome. Frustrated by an elusive sense of masculinity, filled with rage at women for "withholding" the bliss-giving bounty that they believe they possess, man-servants respond by controlling and oppressing women. Why shouldn't they? It bolsters their tarnished self-image by diminishing women's status. It punishes women for being demanding while withholding their bounty. And it puts women, those powerful, ungiving landladies of the treasure man-servants desire, into a subordinate role. Thus, by subduing women, man-servants place themselves in a position to do one of two things: They can either devalue a particular woman's bounty ("no one so insignificant could possibly possess the significant magic of a libidinal bounty"), which provides an excuse for abandoning the inadequate female in order to find one who possesses the libidinal magic; or, alternatively, man-servants can fantasize that once subjugated, a woman obedient to *his* authority will be compelled to surrender the bounty that his best effort was incapable of earning.

Rage and Oppression

Man-servant syndrome brings men's ambivalence toward women into high relief. Men adore women and they trample them. They see them as possessing special redeeming magic and painful, dismembering guile. Women are dauntless adversaries and vulnerable supplicants. They are Virgin Mary and disloyal whore.

In a Brothers Grimm story, "The Fairy Tale of One Who Went Forth to Learn Fear," the hero wants to learn to shudder. He takes on fearful tasks requiring extraordinary courage and strength, but they produce no shudder in him. What finally gives him the shudders is his bride (who, incidentally, he won through great feats). How does she do it? In bed, at night, she throws a pail of cold water filled with minnowlike fish onto him. Covered with icy water and squirming fish, he exclaims that he is shuddering. Small wonder. What is the message here? Men can learn fear from a woman in bed. In bed she possesses power that can transform a hero into a trembling fool, the butt of a joke. The symbolism is marvelously obvious. Women act in the dark. Without warning, they cool the hot promise of libidinal bounty with a frigidity that leaves a man shuddering and covered with limp, dying, tiny fish!

Men who seek women's affirmation of their masculinity end up as vulnerable and foolish as the Brothers Grimm character. These men give women the power to judge whether their efforts qualify them as real men. Because women do not really have the power to make the magically transforming positive judgment, men experience this as a negative judgment. What follows are feelings that, no doubt, would occur if a woman actually dashed ice water on a man's bedroom aspirations. He feels frustration, resentment, and anger at the woman for failing to remove his doubts about his frogness, and at himself for being a repulsive, servile frog. (A woman who awaits Prince Charming has similar experiences. Her negative feelings are directed at men for failing to arrange her coronation as a princess, and at herself for sponsoring psychological suicide.)

Annabel Lazarus is a professional woman. The story that she told me about her first marriage is a tragic, frightening illustration of how deep men's resentment and rage can be.

He treated me like a little girl. That bolstered his own ego. It was to build himself up. . . . Yes, I was the little girl. I had long hair. I'm naive now; I was extremely naive then and as long as I was his little girl, everything was fine.

("What did his little girl do for him?")

Well, we had a good sexual relationship. We went out to dinner a lot. I probably made him feel young. I probably gave him someone he could control. You know, so he could exercise his ego. He was insecure at the time, but I didn't realize it.

(I asked her to tell me what he was insecure about. There were no surprises. She guessed that his concern was about being a man and feeling powerful. Then she went on to tell me how he tried to overcome his concerns. What she said about that was less expected.)

I mean, he controlled every aspect of my behavior. How to dress. How to talk. What to say. What to drink. What kinds of jewelry to wear. Where I worked. I mean, I was stupid! I just turned my entire paycheck over to him and he handled all the finances. I was one of these women who did not know how to write a check. . . . You know, he handled everything, everything!! Later on, when I came to Washington, I found out that I liked to drink rum, gin, and champagne; but while I was with him, I drank bourbon because he used to drink bourbon, with branch water and whatnot. And when I started to grow up, the relationship started to change and it became very combative, and when I started to go to college, it became very difficult. When I met him I'd been working full time and going to school at night. . . . He said not to do it now, he would take care and next year I could go. And it was always next year I could go, and next year I could go, and it just never happened.

(To any onlookers, Annabel explained, her husband seemed anything but full of self-doubt.)

He came on very strongly. He was always the life of the party and the center of attention. I mean he is a . . . was a . . . FABULOUS SPEAKER. Excellent dancer. He had a singing voice . . . played the piano. He just projected a tremendous amount of confidence, optimism, and strength. . . . It's as though it was a screen he was projecting, an image. This was how he wanted to be and he acted that way. But I cannot really explain the drinking {he was an alcoholic} and destructive behavior unless it was because underneath he didn't feel that this image he was projecting and his own self-image were the same thing.

(Annabel told me that things started to change as soon as they got married.)

Before, there was always the possibility that I could walk away. Once we were married, he didn't have to try anymore. . . . Then he started exploring other women.

(I asked Annabel how she knew that he had been unfaithful. She explained that she caught him in the act. What she saw, however, actually tells us something additional about her former husband's control and oppression of women.)

The position I found the woman in, there was no way it could have been the first time. . . . She was tied down to the bed and he had his penis in her mouth. It isn't the sort of position that you jump into on the first day of a beginning love affair. I don't think people do that . . . so he must have been fooling around then, but I don't know for how long. . . .

(The discovery of her husband's indisputable infidelity put a nail into the coffin of Annabel Lazarus, little girl. Her husband was no Prince Charming. She made a move toward self-reliance by deciding to go against his wishes and return to school.)

He was so threatened by my going to school, it was absolutely incredible.

("As soon as you stopped being the little girl he felt threatened.")

Very, very threatened. . . . I had to stop drinking . . . so we didn't have any communication there. And then I cut my hair and he saw that as a form of rebellion, and then I went back to school. . . . When I started to really grow up, we began getting into all kinds of problems. . . . If he hadn't been fooling around, I don't know whether we could have worked those through. . . . But he was terribly, terribly threatened. Really.

Well, by then, when I started college I was twenty-eight. Later—it was the fall semester of my senior year—three or so years later—and we were living out in the boondocks. . . . I had an hour commute to school, and I was getting up very early in the morning. I was working. I was also doing fieldwork. . . . It was holiday time and we got into a big argument about whether I was going to go back to school. He said I couldn't go; I said I had to, and it was only three weeks more. I had term papers. I had exams. In the meantime, a couple of weeks before, he had sold my car. Now, it was my car but it was registered in his name. He said, "No. You're not going back." He had the lock changed on another vehicle and would sleep with the distributor cap of our third car.

(Incredulous, I said, "He slept with a distributor cap?")

Under his pillow. He didn't have to do that because I wouldn't have known how to put it back together if I had had it.

(All this, she said, was to control her. But she was not about to be controlled any longer.)

. . . Monday came and I had to go to school, and so I packed

my books and stuff into a Hefty garbage bag. I had nothing else to carry and it was raining—and I hitched rides to my fieldwork site and then to school. . . . I finished school. . . . I went back after everything was over, but he had cleaned out the house. He had sold everything. . . . EVERYTHING! So I stayed a half hour and I left, and I haven't seen him since.

Defensive oppression. I interviewed Annabel more than a decade after she walked out of that house. By then, she had finished her professional training and had embarked on a career. She was warm and confident, but the scars of her husband's oppression were still evident. As a friend, I wished that they weren't there. But as an interviewer, I recognized that her experiences reflected how man-servant syndrome fuels men's subjugation and abuse of women: Failing in their efforts to experience affirmation, men put the blame on women. Women demand, disappoint, and withhold. Their possession of the desired treasure gives them the power to do so. Men have no choice—women must be corralled, put in their place.

This view of male oppression of women as a defense against women's imagined power finds support in anthropological interpretations of myths and fables from male-dominant cultures around the world. The central theme of these stories is that female subjugation is necessary in order to prevent oppression of men by women, who are characterized as being either dangerously power hungry or incompetent.

I believe that by depicting women in these ways, such stories (which, you must keep in mind, are the products of male-dominant cultures) actually reveal concerns that men in these societies have about themselves. Feeling hungry for power and incompetent because they cannot measure up to the excessively idealized standards of the male competency cluster, these men turn things around 180 degrees and perceive women as power hungry (because I, man, feel weak) and incompetent (because I, man, feel below the cluster's standard).

I should also point out that male dominance tends to occur in societies that live in dangerously inhospitable environments. These are settings that place a premium on traits in the male competency cluster, exaggerating their importance and raising the stakes for "being a *man*." Interestingly, inquiries made by anthropological researchers have shown that men in such societies characterize the inhospitable environmental dangers facing them as *female*. Man's job, then, is to control the dangerous female forces by either subduing or destroying them in order to prevent life-threatening disaster. Certainly, one obvious interpretation of these findings, consistent with the dynamics of man-servant syndrome, is that male dominance is a defensive reaction to the perception that women are powerful in a way that can be harmful to men.

In short, what induces men to subjugate women is their own feeling of vulnerability and self-doubt, not an exploitable weakness in women. Male chauvinism, from this perspective, is nothing more than the political expression of men's disappointment. The disappointment results from men's fantasy that women have the magical bounty to make them feel like "princes" and from men's experience that they've been insufficiently manlike to earn the bounty's surrender.

The truth of this conclusion is demonstrated humorously. You probably know the tired joke that goes, "My wife takes care of the little things like the house, money, vacations, and clothing, while I take care of the important ones like the nation's fiscal policy and trade relationships with third world countries."

Male dominance is a myth that feeds the fantasies of men and women caught up in their respective syndromes. It lets men feel that they are the bosses, providing and protecting, and it allows women to pretend that they are passively subordinate and need men's help. In reality, there is an interpersonal balance of power. Men's formal, external, in-the world power is offset by women's informal, internal between-people power. This doesn't mean that women aren't unfairly cut off from many of society's prizes. They are. Moreover, what they gain through the power that they have may not at all be equal to what they lose. Nonetheless, because men's domination of women rests on the belief that the latter have the, as yet, undelivered power to give them the life that they want, women have counterpower.

For men, women's treasure is not just gently curved and delicate, offering bliss. It is also hard-edged, sharp, and capable of destroying the undefended male psyche. Imagine, if you will, the plight Prince Charming might be in if Sleeping Beauty responded to his wake-up kiss with a yawning grumble about being disturbed, telling him that she's going back to sleep, and why doesn't he go tumble in the thorns for a while longer.

What's a man to do? In order to get the treasure, he feels that it's necessary to prove himself worthy by serving. This is the instrumental part of man-servant's giving. But serving makes him subordinate as well as vulnerable to women's perfidiousness, their withholding, and worse. The solution is to control women. Thus, in addition to being instrumental, man-servant's giving to women is always an effort to control. There is no altruism in the giving. It is never an unalloyed expression of devotion and love.

Women are sometimes fooled by such giving, but not always. They know it to be controlling. They've told me so in interviews, and they've written about it. Toward the end of her marriage, Annabel Lazarus knew it about her husband. Although, up until then he had beguiled her into coming under his control.

Annabel deserves no criticism. Man-servants are adroit at what they do, and there are styles of man-servanting that expertly camouflage the control factor. Such styles offer women a tantalizing promise of a life that little girls dream about. Such sweet bait encourages a big bite: "All the better for hooking you, my dear."

There are three common styles of man-servanting. Each has an exaggerated concern with a different part of the male competency cluster and draws from it its own brand of dangerously sweet bait to dangle in front of women.

First, there are MINISTERS. Ministers focus on that part of the male competency cluster which has to do with *man as provider*. Ministers *do for* women, which to them means becoming capable of being *all-giving*. Their behavior proclaims a desire to *worship* women (the instrumental giving). Ministers put women on pedestals. But the pedestals that they create are narrow, constraining platforms from which the only way off is a long way down.

A second group of man-servants, the EDUCATORS, attend to that part of the male competency cluster which concerns *man's competence and ability*. Educators *do to* women. They interpret the male competency cluster as commanding men to be *all-knowing*. They want to *guide* women in order to improve their lot in life (the instrumental giving). But in order to "guide," educators need students. For them, that means women less competent than they who, therefore, must work very hard to learn what the educators have to teach.

The third kind of man-servant is the LANCELOT. Lancelots are concerned with that part of the male competency cluster which dictates that *men need to be strong and protective.* Lancelots *do in front of* women. For them, the cluster's injunction is to be *all-powerful*, to *dazzle* women with their immense power (the instrumental giving). But in order to display this power, Lancelots need weak women who are in need of protection. There are many differences among these three styles of man-servant: Ministers mind women, educators mold them, and Lancelots master them—but the one thing they have in common is that women who accept their sweet-baited, instrumental giving must also be prepared to accept its terrible price: control.

SERVING STYLES: THE MINISTER - WORSHIPING WOMEN

I'm walking in a park. And it's a very serene and very beautiful park. And I'm asking the question about the universe and the future, and how I can start to reach for becoming my true self. And I encounter in the park a woman, and then another, and a series of women, and they're twelve in all. And each successive woman represents, I guess symbolically, the stages of growth, because at the end of this encounter I become transformed by it.

The dream is John Noblework's. John exhibits elements of Man-Servant Syndrome, Style: Minister. As is the case with other man-servant ministers, John endows women with goddesslike qualities. He portrays them as possessing unusual perfection, purity, and power, places them on pedestals, and then behaves as if worship, sacrifice, adoration, and reverence are their due. Indeed, man-servant ministers like John seem convinced that women/god-desses' bounty will not be given, and their own transfor-mation into a "complete man" will not occur without this homage.

Serving

For man-servant ministers, the key to receiving women/goddesses' redeeming bounty is to *do for* them. Conse-quently, these men provide. They do good acts. They are kind, courteous, unselfish, and understanding. Ministers fetch and follow, never feeling satisfied that what they've done is enough. More could have been done, and what was done could have been done better. Feeling something less than number one, they try harder, and *do* still more.

Serving is the hallmark of man-servant ministers' instru-mental giving. This is the behavior that they believe wins women. By placing women on pedestals, where they can be worshiped, honored, revered, catered to, and sacrificed for, man-servant ministers try to earn the goddesses' magically transforming bounty.

John Noblework's thoughts after he first met his future wife tell the story as well as it can be told:

I remember thinking that she was not a person for me because, for one, she was much too beautiful. I mean, a really stunning woman. . . . And she had what I considered to be all the major attributes. . . . In a sense, you could say I was looking for someone with whom I would have a role in her life. . . . I thought she could have anybody she wanted. That she was super-independent, and intelligent, and accomplished, and that she could do pretty much what she wanted. I felt like I was in a different league. . . .

In fact, I remember one conversation—she was talking about her divorce [note: She was leaving what John saw as a very abusive relationship]. . . . *I guess the gist of it was she was concerned about not finding decent men and this kind of thing. And I talked to her about a guy* [someone they both knew] . . . *and said, "Hey, I've talked with both of you and there's some interesting stuff going on, on both sides"—similar stages of development, and I encouraged her to go out with him.*

(I alluded to the Pilgrim John Alden, who was told by Priscilla Mullins to speak for himself. John Noblework accepted the interruption graciously, and went on talking about the woman/goddess whom he'd met.)

In any case, I don't know what caused the transition. . . . After a while I started to fall in love with her. I knew that one dimension of preparation that I had that she didn't have is what I'd call an active spiritual life.

(He was going to win her by providing gifts that were a product of his quest for personal goodness. The initial results were positive.)

She found me attractive because of what she perceived to be an inner goodness, a kind of person, a man who was after some pretty moral things. I wasn't sleeping with her or even trying anything like that. She was looking for somebody who was, I guess, a different class of person. Because of her physical beauty she had lots of opportunities.

Special, goddesslike women require special, godlike men. Through acts of goodness and devotion, man-servant ministers work hard to prove their worthiness. Ultimately, ministers are their own worst critics. By their own efforts, their wish to ascend Olympus is denied. The requirements of the male competency cluster that they have set for themselves prove to be excessive.

Ministers are seekers of an affirmative answer to the question "Am I a good provider?" As is true for all man-servants, whatever their style, the standards that they are trying to achieve are elusive. In the special case of ministers, no matter how much they *do for* women, and regardless of how much loving joy women may put into their response, doubts persist and the ministers never feel satisfied. Being really good is always just beyond the ministers' grasp. In the end, they deal with their disappointment by punishing both themselves and the women who they turned into goddesses.

Blaming

If man-servant ministers had a crest, then written boldly across it might be the words GAIN THROUGH SACRIFICE. With their bankbooks and in their bedrooms, ministers sacrifice to their women/goddesses and then lie back, sometimes literally, waiting for a gain that will redeem them. What happens next is predictable: no gain . . . real pain . . . whose to blame?

Let's make a deal. John Noblework told me how his bankbook became a sacrificial altar. It started just before he and Barbara were going to be married.

She told me about how she had not been able to fulfill our agreement about paying off her debts. . . . And that she really, in fact, couldn't join me without doing that. So, I gave her the money. I wrote her a check for whatever it was. A couple of grand, I guess.
Now, I had been working hard to kind of take care of my debts

and manage money better. I had some bucks and some things I hadn't done, but I felt pretty confident it was going to be all right.

(An event followed that shook John's confidence.)

Things started coming apart in her life. The next thing that happened, I paid all the wedding expenses. And that was O.K. But I started to get really anxious because it was just this feeling— I was giving and giving. And then something else that happened was, after we got married, during the honeymoon, I gave her three or four gifts, she didn't have any gifts for me. I don't even know if she thought about it. We hadn't talked about it . . . but it just seemed like, well, I noticed the imbalance in the giving, if you know what I mean.

(Another event occurred that turned John's shaken confidence into what he described as a sense of "growing annoyed." I don't think that he was simply "growing annoyed." It sounded to me as if John was plain angry. But man-servant ministers don't like to admit that they can be as nasty to their women/goddesses as the word "angry" implies. So let's say that, because of what happened next, John was "growing annoyed.")

. . . It started to set up this notion that I'm responding to her needs and I'm waiting in abeyance for . . . mine to be addressed. . . . Even if the material circumstances of her life didn't permit her to—even if I, in sharing with her, handled the monetary part of it, the balance would have been more or less symbolic, a token gift based on her situation. Sort of a continuation of what I felt was someone who was interested in me and wanted to understand where I hurt and what I felt, and what my dreams were . . . and all of that would help to bring me out and help me to grow spiritually . . . find a way to gently remind me of my greatness {chuckle}, so to speak.

*　　*　　*

John Noblework hoped that this special woman would respond to his devotion by *gently reminding him of his greatness.* He was "annoyed" that she hadn't caressed his brow with the warm oil of anointment. His sacrifice was unsuccessful. He was going to have to search for other ways to be reminded of his greatness.

The erotic minister. For many man-servant ministers, the search for other ways to experience their greatness takes place in the bedroom. In general, the bedroom equals the bankbook as a crucible in which man-servants' experiences with women are tested. In the bedroom, man-servants give, each according to his own style, but cannot receive from women.

First, man-servants cannot receive from women because what they want is fantastic, way beyond any mortal woman's ability to give. Second, their ability to receive is impaired by their own efforts to *do for* (the ministers), *to* (the educators), or *in front of* (the Lancelots) women during lovemaking. Believing that they are being caring (the ministers), helpful (the educators), or skillful lovers (the Lancelots), men from all three groups end up being self-conscious and unspontaneous. Rather than being participants, they become observers of their own lovemaking.

The third and final reason man-servants cannot receive from women is because they see a woman's lovemaking as repayment for what they have done, not as a gift, freely given and spontaneous. The result is that man-servants are "on duty," and bedrooms are not a totally fun place for them to be.

In my psychotherapy practice, I worked with a call girl. On one occasion this woman explained to me that in her professional experience she met three kinds of men. None of them, she observed, were doing anything more than masturbating in the company of a woman. According to her analysis, a woman was an essential stimulus to the man's arousal—in the way that an erotic picture might be—but to him, she was not really a partner who also experiences and receives.

The first kind of men she described (the ministers) were aroused by being "gentlemen" with her. She explained her use of the word "gentlemen" by telling me that these men told her how she was really a good person who did not deserve the life that she led. They tried, she said, to be very decent. For man-servant ministers, erotic stimulation comes from *giving*.

She continued by saying that a second group (the educators), before, during, and after their sexual encounter, carried on about how they would show her things. Sometimes they claimed, "I'll bet you never did this with your clients." (She assured me that she always did.) Or they encouraged her to "use this next time." ("Use it next time!" she exclaimed. "Hell, I use it all the time.") The educators become aroused by *teaching*.

The third group (the Lancelots) tried to shock and dazzle her with their size, endurance, strength, or athleticism. They pinned her down, thrust hard, and asked her whether she "could take more." Lancelots are aroused by their own *performance*.

Some man-servant ministers told me about their erotic fantasies. These fantasies have a common core that reveals these men's orientation toward women. Man-servant ministers are titillated by the *Rescue Fantasy*. This fantasy has three components: (1) A maiden is captured by brutes (other men) who are intent on ravishing her. (2) The minister, with a pure heart, rescues her. (3) She recognizes him as special and does things to make him feel very good.

I heard the following story from Timothy Biwant, a twenty-nine-year-old hospital administrator.

I used to think of Elaine all of the time—at night—before I fell asleep. She was really lovely. Actually, I never did anything—dated or really spoke to her very much. I doubt that she knew what I had for her. She was like—fine—you know—fragile—very special—fresh. She was in the park. This is my dream, fantasy. She was in the park and these guys grab her. Bad buys. Really kind of low-lifes. Like pirates or something. Except there are no pirates in the park. Anyway, they have her naked, on the ground. Not doing anything yet. Then I come along and somehow they go away. It's really not clear. I don't know how that happens. No fight. They just sort of go away. Do they run or what? It doesn't matter.

(I wondered, in silence, about whether it does matter. Maybe it matters a great deal. Maybe the bad guys are actually him. Maybe he feels that he's bad because he'd like to do to women what these "pirates" were doing to Elaine. Perhaps the *doing for* is a way for him to deny or disguise his desire to ravish them. Or maybe it's as compensation for these "bad" desires that he wants to provide for women, put them on pedestals, and prove his decency by worshiping them. Could it be that man-servant ministers are trying to do good just because they feel that they are bad?

Timothy continued.)

I cover her and hold her. She's actually so grateful and fright-

ened that she sorts of holds me—gestures to me to hold her. She recognizes that I wouldn't do what they did. So that she's pleased and kind of holds me and walks with me. She's like mine. It's heaven.

The Elaine of Timothy's fantasy recognizes his worth and sacrifice. Heaven is his reward. It's a place where "good" people go. Any sense of doubt about his worth—which may, in fact, have been the very reason that he kept away from this "fine, fragile, very special, fresh" woman in the fantasy—is momentarily whisked away by her fantasized embrace.

The Rescue Fantasy reflects the man-servant ministers' problems and also adds to them. The standards are set too high. And because they are, man-servant ministers are often so severely disappointed in themselves and in their women/goddesses that their adoring, worshipful efforts become cruelly oppressive.

Oppression

This dangerous roundabout pathway into oppression is illustrated by a conversation that I had with a leading corporate executive. I regard him as someone with unusual sensitivity, psychological savvy, and personal daring. The relevant point in our conversation came when he told me about his decision to marry Marisa. He said:

. . . Maybe I was looking back to my old dream of having a . . . nurturing female [with me] as the center of all attention.
 (That didn't quite fit with things that he'd said earlier in

the conversation, so I asked, "How does that fit with putting her on a pedestal?" He'd actually used the word "pedestal," I wasn't planting the thought in his mind.)

Well, the pedestal. You know . . . I don't know. Let me just think. You picked up a very good point. {Pause} In the past, women were put up on pedestals by society. My own version of a woman came a lot from Hollywood; came a lot from reading romantic novels; and a woman was on a pedestal in terms of being untouchable.

I couldn't conceive of a woman going to the bathroom when I was a kid, O.K.? They were goddesslike. They smelled and looked beautiful, and I was a very strong romantic as a child. . . . Marisa and I were just talking about it yesterday. It was really amusing. There was a girl by the name of Ruby Scheffield that I fell in love with when I was eleven. I loved her for three years. In fact, we {he and Marisa} were watching the U.S.A., Miss U.S.A. contest, and the Texas gal that won yesterday reminded me of Ruby Scheffield. She had that extraordinary beauty: beautiful blue eyes, shiny and glowing. You know, a woman—this kind of woman on a pedestal, a beauty, being goddesslike, doesn't sweat—you know the old cliché, they glow. They don't even perspire, they glow. And so, there is a sense of pedestal as being something special and Hollywood did a lot for that.

(He told me that he no longer lived with the illusion. But it took him a long time to realize that "Hollywood was a total farce." During the time he believed in it, however, he confessed that he had exaggerated expectations of what a woman could do for a man.)

Women could do special things at creating happiness for you as a man. But it was always a man at the center . . . the Cinderella story just occurred to me, spontaneously, of the fairy godmother—

she would be around and touch you and things. It would be
wonderful for you. You'd come back and you'd have this wonderful
castlelike home.

Perhaps it is just because man-servant ministers cannot
imagine the idea of even ordinary odors coming from their
women/goddesses, that eventually they are revolted by a
woman who "pretended" to be a goddess but actually
smells very human. These women are flawed, false idols
who lack a state of grace and therefore do not deserve the
pedestals that they are placed upon. Comforted by the ral-
lying cry "After all that I did for her!" the man-servant
ministers run off in search of a "real" goddess for whom
they can *do.*

In time, it is always the pointed truth of reality that
bursts the ministers' balloons. When the inevitable occurs
and there is no anointment, ministers find themselves
grappling yet again, with questions about their worth.
How should they interpret what happened? There was
sacrifice, but no gain. The goddess did not anoint them.

When they don't blame women for their disappointment,
man-servant ministers often interpret the failure to receive
and be transformed by a woman's rapturous bounty as additional proof of their own unworthiness. What happens
next is as predictable as it is tragic. Guided by the idea that
unworthy people need to be penitent in order to be re-
deemed, man-servant ministers do penance by sacrificing
still more. But it's all a sham. Peel back the camouflage and
what you find is that ministers conveniently sacrifice in ways
that punish the ungiving women/goddesses who have disappointed them.

Let's start with the self-blame part. Fred Sapman's story

shows how far this can go. Fred stands out in a crowd. He is a couple of inches more than six feet tall, red-haired, with the build of a committed athlete. Just after they were married, he and his wife began full-time study for their MBAs. Within the year, Fred's wife had an affair with one of their professors. Fred knew about it almost as soon as it happened. They stayed married for nearly ten years and several affairs after that, at which point she finally ended their marriage legally. When I spoke with Fred about the first affair and his marriage, the only tarnish he could see was on his self-image.

She had an affair with one of our professors and it was devastating for me. It was really painful, and still is. I mean, it was incredible at the time. It happened mostly because, I think, she was somewhat unhappy and felt kind of isolated.

(I asked Fred to tell me what she was unhappy about and why she felt isolated.)

We lived away from the center of things. . . . I think she was confused and unhappy. It wasn't anything. In our relationship there was mostly positive stuff—as I saw it.

In any case, I forgave that, and over time we were starting to rebuild a relationship. What happened, happened because I really didn't understand her priorities—where we lived, you know. Maybe I was too goal-directed—concentrating. I'm not sure but more attention—well, we were spending time—I just don't know but maybe I didn't do enough.

Man-servant ministers begin and end relationships with women in the same psychological place. They wonder about their worth as providers. But during the course of the relationships, by *doing for* women, they receive short-term relief from the nagging concern about their worth. After all,

A KNIGHT IN SHINING ARMOR 57

how can their worthiness be questioned if they are trying to be decent? Anyone observing their relationship would say, "He worshiped her. There was nothing that he wouldn't do. No sacrifice was too much."

No doubt disappointment follows the short-term relief. Women have no means of repaying the ministers' sacrifices by providing them with absolution from self-doubt. Even this disappointment, however, fits into the man-servant ministers' scheme of things. It proves their unworthiness, thereby providing the motive power for them to be penitent by *doing more for* women. In the end, however, as they *do for* women more and more, less and less are women allowed to do for themselves. The result is that women's sense of dependency, helplessness, and obligation grows. Stifling, smothering, and controlling are useful descriptions of man-servant ministers' behavior as experienced by women. For them, the providing deprives to the point of oppression.

Listen closely to the words of a woman who once loved a man-servant minister until she found herself oppressed because she was up on the pedestal without any way of getting down.

This guy did everything for me. Lovely. It was lovely. So lovely. Right? My parents—everyone—friends, except one, she was smart—they envied me. "He's so good." I can't believe that I could have liked it so. For God's sake, I was no kid: twenty-seven. I was really attracted to it. It was like a dream—nightmare, really. A real decent guy. So kind. I mean, I'm successful, independent. How could it have been so whatever? My God, it was icky. He was like damned molasses: sweet, but icky. I couldn't move after a while. And you know I felt guilty. Can you believe it? He made me feel guilty. To go out for a walk by myself—buy a magazine—

friends—anything. If I said no—if I did my own thing—I felt guilty. He was so-ooo good. I owed him—felt like I did. Felt so guilty. I was stuck, STUCK, STUCK, up on a pedestal and he had the damned ladder.

Man-servant educators and Lancelots, too, manage their disappointment over not receiving a woman's bounty by becoming oppressive. Of course, these men oppress in ways that are suitable to their style of man-servanting.

SERVING STYLES: THE EDUCATOR— GUIDING WOMEN

As I write this chapter, I find myself thinking about Annabel Lazarus. Her sad, angry words about her marriage are so appropriate, they beg to be repeated here.

I mean, he controlled every aspect of my behavior. How to dress. How to talk. What to say. What to drink. What kinds of jewelry to wear. Where I worked. I mean, I was stupid!

I never met Annabel Lazarus's husband, but her tormenting experience of feeling "stupid" is typical of women who are in relationships with men suffering from Man-Servant Syndrome, Style: Educator. By using constant criticism and correction as levers, these men adroitly pry away at a woman's doubts and vulnerabilities, ripping apart her confidence and making her feel "stupid."

While I never met Annabel's husband, I did interview a fellow whom I'll call Maurice Mandar, and I've no doubts

59

about Maurice. He certainly exhibits elements of Man-Servant Syndrome, Style: Educator. I hardly had time to take a breath after finishing the introduction to my interview with him, when he said:

Well, I think probably the easiest place to start is with my first marriage, which was to a woman who was six or seven years younger than me—just graduating from college—from a family with a great deal less education. More of a working class than I was. I represented a kind of savoir-faire, *intellectual glamour, and I loved it. . . . That made me feel really important. . . . There's a certain appeal for me in that kind of neediness. That's part of nurturing and caretaking and bringing along and so on.*

(He then did an imitation of his first wife, paraphrasing what she seemed to be saying to him when they first met.)

". . . Well, I really don't know how to make myself into anything. I really don't seem to be much of anything."

(Maurice concluded this performance by speaking as himself again.)

Here's someone who not only needs it, but is asking for it!

(He continued by telling me why this woman was appealing to him.)

. . . My fantasy was that this young woman, who was from a lower-class, working-class background, who was the first in her family to go to college and had gone to a local community college—it was not on a high intellectual level—she was, through me, going to become an educated, cultured person with all the interest of the middle class or more. I don't know if she particularly wanted that.

(To get into the conversation, as much as for any other reason, I inquired, "There was never an indication on her part that that was something she desired?")

I think that she liked being around someone who represented that, but I don't think that she had—you know, when push came to shove, and I think the history of the relationship indicates, when push came to shove [pay attention to the language here], *she didn't want to be* **brought along** *in quite the way I had in mind.*

She didn't want to become a clone of me or a clone of my fantasy of what the cultured woman of the sixties was like. . . . She was adventurous and liked looking into things that she had not seen before. But the fact that it was interesting to go to an excellent French restaurant didn't mean that she was going to change her taste in food, which—her preference was fried chicken and a can of beer—was gonna pretty much remain the same and that was fine with her.

I really had an image of who I was, which was a little inflated, and an image of how much better it was to be like me than to be like her, and I was going to save her, to help her by helping her to be like me.

Man-servant educators replace the perfection, purity, and power that man-servant ministers attribute to women with a view of them as incompetent, disabled underachievers. Educators treat women as if they need to be hoisted to their feet and supported, and want men to do it for them. Educators do not put women on pedestals where their attributes can be worshiped. Rather, through word and deed, educators focus on the inadequacies they see in women. Their only aim, these men proclaim, is to help women realize their real potential by making up for their unfortunate lacks. The educator's fantasy is that when women's transformation is complete, and they have been helped to reach some undefined (and therefore unreachable) level of development, women will then be able to give their bounty to the educator. Even more important, women will want to give him that bounty because they will owe everything they are to the educator's competent service.

Serving

For man-servant educators, the key to acquiring women's bounty is to *do to* women. These men act as if women are diamonds in the rough for whom transformation into sparkling gems occurs only through the intervention of a man's competent hand. In their own eyes, educators see themselves as developing, teaching, and advancing women.

The cornerstone of the educator's instrumental giving is his view of women: They are inadequate but, like children, they have potential. "Potential," however, is a matter for the future. Today's reality is that women don't know about the world and are incompetent to manage in it. Therefore, to an educator, what women need and desire is to have men improve their lot in life by taking them on as protégées and giving them the opportunity to acquire the abilities that they lack.

The protégée problem. Steven Galli's story is a typical one.

O.K. My first marriage . . . I was a research chemist working for a company and I met my then future wife because she was working for the same company in a clerical position and, after a fairly short, y'know, like maybe a year and a half, we decided— actually, I decided to get married.

(Wanting him to say more about that decision, I rephrased the key words in a questioning tone. *"You decided?"* I said.)

I decided. I mean the cards were all in my hands. She was much younger than I was. About seven years, as a matter of fact—and immature. [As it happens, this "immaturity" is just one of several examples of inadequacy that man-servants, particularly educators, typically see in the women that they are with.] *A high school graduate, sexually attractive, and so, we did indeed get married. And some of the things that attracted me to her early turned out later to be the very things that . . . I decided I didn't want to be a part of anymore.*

(When educators' efforts fail to turn their diamond-in-the-rough protégées into bounty-giving gems, they commonly decide that their choice of protégée was an error and they leave to enroll new protégées.)

And those qualities were things like her immaturity, her innocence [take note of what he says next], ***her need to be developed.*** *And I thought that this was good. I could be the teacher—take her to places she had never been before and probably wouldn't have been if I had not married her. Or, at least I had a relationship with her. So, my role became one of developer, teacher, exposing her to experiences—trips to San Francisco for concerts—and—*[that were] *much more sophisticated than her background had previously been.*

She'd lived in a small town. . . . I don't think she had been to any state except Indiana. So [she led] *a very protected life. Her family was Irish Catholic.* [She had a] *very strict upbringing. A very sheltered sort of life. . . . And, therefore, she was somewhat, I don't want to overstate this, but somewhat hero-worshiping around me.*

*   *   *

Man-servant educators, like Steven Galli, are primarily concerned with the competence portion of the male competency cluster. They are seeking an affirmative answer to the question "Am I a competent man?" And they briefly find it by selecting a woman whom they see as inferior.

Believing that they are with incompetent women provides educators with the illusion that they can safely exercise their own competency. A woman's imagined incompetence permits educators to set aside their doubts about how successful they have been in achieving the cluster's demanding, forever elusive standard. Every time educators are able to guide, criticize, and correct women, it inflates their sense of competence because, on those occasions, they are comparing whatever abilities they have to the inferior ones they attribute to women.

Steven Galli's experiences are prototypical of man-servant educators. He tried to produce a positive answer to the core question "Am I a competent man?" by getting together with a woman whom he viewed as not competent and, consequently, needy of what he had to offer. By "guiding" her, he fostered her dependence and sense of inability, while simultaneously providing himself with fodder essential to continuing his illusion of superior competence.

In the end, however, Steven Galli and other man-servant educators as well create a dilemma that prevents them from giving themselves a final passing grade in "competency." In order to get the magical, affirming bounty, they need to have a woman who is a gem, not disabled, needy, and incompetent. But at the same time, they cannot permit their diamond-in-the rough protégées really to shine. If that were to happen, what would the educators do? Their feeling of safety in their relationships with women is contingent on women's continuing lack of competence. It is a trap: Unless women change, educators cannot get the bounty that they incorrectly imagine women possess. But if women do change, it threatens educators' illusions of superior competence. Change or no, educators find reason to conclude that their choice of protégée was a mistake that must be corrected.

Blaming

I have suggested that a crest for man-servant ministers might be emblazoned with the words GAIN THROUGH SACRIFICE. For man-servant educators, the words might be GAIN THROUGH GUIDING.

These are nice-sounding mottoes, but both are false. "There is no gain." The educators' pseudoguidance results in the same tragic outcomes as the ministers' pseudosacrifice: first, disillusionment, then blame, and finally, rage and oppression of women.

Skilled teachers are joyful when their students grow more competent, develop independence, and engage issues in original ways. For man-servant educators, these accomplishments by their protégées produce no such joy.

I asked Steven Galli about his first wife, "When you two had troubles, what were they about?"

Most of the troubles revolved around, well, I'll tell you, two or three different things. One was intellectual stimulation. She was not terribly bright.

(It struck me that in criticizing her intellectual ability, he might have been projecting onto her, doubts that he had about himself. This thought remained with me as I mentioned to him that her innocence and naiveté were the qualities that initially attracted him to her.)

Yes, that's exactly right. Remember, I said that the things that drew me to her later became problems. She was not a reader. I was. She was not a student. I was. And so from an intellectual stimulation standpoint, it was a mismatch. Uh . . . so things that I wanted to talk about, she was unprepared to discuss, or couldn't, or whatever. So, that was quite a problem. For whatever reason, and I'm not quite sure what it was—originally, I'd say that it could have been me, or it could have been her—but I became the very dominant figure in the family. I made the decisions. I decided what we were going to do—where we were going for vacation—it was kind of like I made the decisions and she carried them out. And it became very burdensome.

. . . And, as I say, I may have created this. Looking back on it, I probably did, as a matter of fact. But we colluded, I'm sure. Which came first, the dependency or the dominance, I don't really know. But I do know that it developed over time. It became objectionable to her.

(I wasn't surprised to learn that Steven's wife eventually objected to her subservient role, but I wanted to know what she did to lead him to that observation. Even more, I wanted to learn what *he* did in response to a rebellious protégée.)

She'd say, "No, I don't want to do that." I'd say, "Let's go see my parents for vacation." "I really don't want to see those folks." "What is it that you want to do?" "Well, I want to go someplace else." And where's that? And, you know, maybe visit some of her folks, or go to some seaside place, or go on a family outing with HER folks, with her relatives. So, there was some rebellion on her part. I didn't particularly like her family. I liked her father a lot, but that was as far as it went.

("You didn't like the rebellion?")

No, not really.

("And you didn't like the burden of making all the decisions either?")

Yes, that's right.

(Thinking that by then she was in a tough situation, since he had disapproved of both her dependence and her independence, I asked, "So there wasn't much left?")

It's a hell of a dilemma, ain't it?

The erotic educator. It is a "hell of a dilemma," one that doesn't only concern decisions about vacations, French restaurants, and books. It inserts itself into the bedroom and affects the man-servant educator's sex life.

In contrast to the ministers' erotic *Rescue Fantasy,* educators have a *Pygmalion Fantasy.* Its essence is simple: The educator meets a woman whose life is in some way deprived. For example, these men told me about fantasies in which they had relations with women in poverty, abused women, sheltered women, and (for white males) minority women. Sometimes the fantasy was about a co-worker who had to do a job and desperately needed *his* help, or about a female neighbor who just could not manage life's problems. Whatever the lack, the man has the competence to serve. He shows her how to manage better, she's grateful, and it's happiness forever after. John Denton's daydream is a typical example:

It's a little—strange—awkward—not that I'm ashamed of the sex part—but it's—there's racial stuff that I don't understand. There's this neighbor—not now, but a while ago, several years— she was older—Hispanic. I don't know from where, but anyway Hispanic. She spoke Spanish. My thought was that she'd need help sometime. Actually, she was not that great-looking, but there was—something—attracting—I don't—So I'd help.

("How would you help?" I asked.)

Maybe, first with things she couldn't understand, or telephone calls, or something—it varied. Then she'd want to learn more and we'd sit together. I had like these cushions backed into a couch. She'd struggle like—not know or whatever—a mistake—then I'd pat her hand. You know, "It's O.K." That's how it'd begin. Then it'd go on. She'd look up to me—like I could do things and we'd have this wild sex life.

Note how the fantasy keeps the woman's progress ambiguous, but features her errors and, therefore, her continuing inadequacy. Fantasies are terrific. They give you what you want (in this case, the "wild sex life") without any price tag.

Oppression

But fantasy isn't reality. Educators create a dilemma that has a very serious price. Either they are with a woman who makes changes that challenge their claim to superior competence, or they are with one whose lack of change makes her contemptible, because she doesn't have a bounty worth working for.

Faced with either of these two kinds of women, some educators opt for increasing what they *do to* her. In this way, they send the same signal to women who have been "learning" from their lessons and to those who haven't. The message is simple: *"Despite my best efforts you, woman, are really still incompetent, bumbling, and childlike. Therefore, at great cost to myself, I must continue your education."*

A woman with whom I spoke told me the following:

It's never-ending. I'm too heavy—my buttocks. My conversation is inane. Tennis, golf, nothing do I do well. Once he lectured me on laughing too loudly—at a party—it was after the party— "Laughing should not be an auditory burden to anyone else." I really do not know what to do. This party that we're doing—he knows how to do it all. After I do it—then he corrects me. I should have ordered more. "No one eats cheese puffs anymore." I'm afraid to do anything. To tell you true, when he comes home I get stiff— like a cop walked into the house. He's quiet, you know, but that's not it—I feel like a dummy, a criminal who needs to walk the straight and narrow.

Other educators, when confronted with either women who change and challenge or with those who do not, take a different path. They find the costs too great. Rather than opt to increase what they *do to* a woman, they simply opt out of the relationship.

Eva Moore listened to her man-servant husband's advice to change from an "ordinary housewife"—as she quoted him saying—to a working woman. He didn't enjoy getting what he asked for:

. . . I was doing just what I was brought up to do. As I mentioned, I'm a [she named one of the Seven Sisters Schools] *graduate. Michael was attractive. I was living in Chicago when we met—after I graduated . . . teaching, you know. He'd finished law school and, really, had a promising career. We moved to* [she mentioned a metropolitan area] *immediately after marrying. . . . There was the house in the suburbs, three kids, two cars, one dog, then two dogs, the **club**. It was a picturebook, fairy-tale*

sort of thing. Now, this was the late sixties, early seventies. I had the kids and the house—there was a maid—my friends. Michael traveled a lot, but—as I look back—he took care of everything. . . . I can't say that I fit the stereotype of—you know—not being able to balance a checkbook, but I came close. And I have to say that after all that happened, even today, I find too many women in that position.

Around that time—I don't know why—Michael started to push me to continue my education. Pressure. [She gestured downward, using the flat of her hand, as if something underneath were being squashed.] *He decided that I should go for an MBA, got the material—application, brochures. . . . To tell you the truth, Harvey, it never seemed to me that I thought much about the decision. I don't regret it—the decision—I **am** embarrassed—uncomfortable about how it happened. I would say that what happened around that is typical of how we related. And I have to accept much of the blame—at least around this part of our relationship—the kind of teacher-student, typical, stereotypic sort of thing. . . .*

Be that as it may, I started school, with much advice and instruction and, I have to say, support from him.

I loved it, much more than I thought—could have imagined— and did it very well. Now, all this time he continued his traveling and weekend activity—tennis, golf, although he's not very social. He doesn't like it. I do, but he can be very charming and is on boards of this and that. Privately, he's quite critical of people. No one, especially me, is as smart as he. Oh, perhaps I should add, he's never really approved of how the children were raised. I'm much easier than he. Now they're grown. I feel close to them. He doesn't . . . and that's sad.

The point I want to make is that he continued with his thing and I had to go to school and continue doing everything that I was doing.

When I was finishing school, he spoke about business ideas that he had for me. . . . I believe that [she mentioned the name of her business] *was my idea, originally. He thinks that it was his. I started it in 1977 and, as they say, "The rest is history." It's been very successful.*

("What was his response to the success?")

Well, I'll be honest here, although it's painful. It's important to say. He's still—remains critical. Either I don't do it right, or he could have done it better.

(She paused. I looked up. Nothing that she'd said thus far sounded very "painful." Eva seemed to understand what I was thinking. She nodded and continued speaking.)

I think that's when he started to see other women. There have been a couple—I think. One I know of for sure—young, pretty, and probably was—is?—very much under his wing. Just as I once was.

Steven Galli didn't philander, but he opted out of the relationship with his wife. From his point of view, this part of the story begins with what happened between him and his wife after he was fired from his job. Losing one's job is an experience that can undermine anyone's confidence in their competence. But for man-servant educators, it is a particularly painful experience. It strikes them just where they are most vulnerable.

. . . This is really the first failure I had in my life. And, as a matter of fact, it's the only real major one. Well, that and the ultimate divorce. Even though, very frankly, that was not a failure. That was a {laughter} a releasing thing, a freeing thing. . . . Not to say that everything was always onward and upward, but I had not been totally rejected by whatever it was I

was trying to do—and it just wounded the hell out of me. I was powerless to do anything about it for quite a while . . . impotent. . . . So what did I need at that time? I needed somebody to talk to. Somebody to share this agony with. Somebody to say this is what is happening with me. This is what I'm feeling like. And I didn't have anyone.

But anyway, she was not a sounding board, not someone I could talk to. Communication by that time—and this was maybe fifteen . . . seventeen years into the relationship—there was none. No help there to heal my wounded spirit. So, I think that was the beginning of the end.

I don't really agree with Steven Galli's final observation. The beginning of the end was when he courted this woman because she was, to him, needy and dependent. The end was shaped by events during the nearly two decades of their marriage: events like Steven deciding that they would get married; his telling her to go to school; and, by his saying, "Make something more of yourself," while he nurtured her subservience. And the end became all but certain when Steven's wife stepped out of her passivity and voiced objections to Steven's "guidance."

In fact, her inability to respond to his crisis and "heal his wounded spirit" (give him the soothing, emotional salve of a woman's bounty), which he thinks of as the "beginning of the end," was really only another milestone on the path that he and his wife started marking out nearly twenty years earlier. What she was by the time of this crisis was something that Steven Galli, man-servant educator, had helped create.

Men experiencing Man-Servant Syndrome, Style: Educator trap themselves into failing relationships with women.

The final tragic reality for them is that their own sense of competence is dependent on "guiding" women to greater competence. However, whether they are with "guidable" women or not hardly matters: Women who demonstrate "guidability" become too great a threat, while those who do not demonstrate "guidability" are barren—without the bounty. They earn the educators' contempt. The truth is that no woman is capable of giving educators the secure sense of competence that they want. As Steven Galli said, "It's a hell of a dilemma, ain't it?"

SERVING STYLES: THE LANCELOT - DAZZLING WOMEN

For a while Jack Able puzzled me. He clearly showed signs of man-servant syndrome, but there was no clear evidence of a predominant style. This lack of clarity didn't bother me. Nearly eighty interviews had preceded Jack's, and I'd already learned that more often than not, men evidenced a mixture of three styles—minister, educator, and Lancelot; only a few were pure types. But every man I spoke with had a preferred style of dealing with women, and every woman I interviewed easily described the predominant style of man-servanting the men that they knew used.

At first, Jack Able sounded a bit like a minister:

Let me start just by going way back—as I became aware of man-woman relationships. I guess I'm a very good example of the guy that belongs to the previous generation. Where I put women on a pedestal. My feeling was, while I went to school, females were, in general, actually better than the males in school.

(Despite the sound of that opening statement, it rapidly became clear that Jack was no minister. What he had to say next had an entirely different ring to it.)

It was later that males moved into their own and they sort of took over the running of society, if you will. And the female really took care of the home. I still have—although substantially changed in many areas—the feeling that the female's role of a traditional nature of the past is still very important in today's world. . . . Yeah, this nest business, to me, is very, very important.

In Jack Able's world, women watch from the nest while men "move into their own" and, following what Jack sees as the natural order of things, "take over the running of society." To me, Jack Able was sounding very much like someone with Man-Servant Syndrome, Style: Lancelot.

Lancelots take over, manage, and protect. They joust with other men, seek prestigious positions, and take risks. By either building or destroying, they work to alter the physical environment. Lancelots perform in order to titillate, excite, and lure women. They hope that because of their macho deeds the *me* a woman sees will be the powerful and therefore, to their way of thinking, alluring figure a man must be in order to win a woman's bounty. Lancelots embrace a "to the winner goes the spoils" mentality, which depicts women as "the spoils": Women are powerless, passive pawns who automatically give their affirming, magical favor to the knight with the winning lance.

One young man with whom I spoke, an actor in his early twenties, told me: *Women are attracted to my self-confidence. I can be a protector. This past weekend I was sitting on a bench with a woman. (We spent the weekend together.) There were some black men nearby. You know how black men can sometimes assault an attractive black woman with their eyes. It's really heavy. Sexy. But I tell you, you know, that doesn't happen if they're with me. I'm a buffer—a border guard. I keep the boundary.*

Serving

I asked Jack Able what a man had to do in order to get a woman's favors.

You'd have to be pretty attractive to her, whatever that is— sensitive, good-looking. As a kid, I was a pretty cute kid. I remember—I'll call it the way I feel it, which was really funny. . . . It sounds self-serving. I looked like a cute little Latino kid. And for some reason girls always liked me. When I was five years old, six years old, I always ended up playing doctor. {Laughter} And . . . and part of that, I think, attracted April: that I was sort of cute. Other girls liked me and that tends to go for teenagers, young kids, you know, that's part of it.

Man-servant Lancelots perform. They *do in front of* women, displaying their wares and hoping for an affirmative answer to the question "Am I a powerful man?" Lancelots' deeds are not a product of personal conviction about their manhood. These men do not take over, manage, protect, risk, or alter the world because they feel macho. On the contrary, Lancelots use deeds like these to secure affirmative answers to questions they have about just how powerful they really are. They offer these deeds to women hoping that women will find the offerings acceptable and signal that acceptance by giving them their affirming bounty. That is the affirmation Lancelots seek. (Of course, the irony is that no matter how great their victories, because Lancelots depend on women to affirm their power as men, they remain plagued by a sense of vulnerability and doubt about how successful they really are.)

Whispering, as if he were telling me a secret, Jack Able spoke for all man-servant Lancelots when he said:

Ecstasy, ecstasy. I've known ecstasy. Absolute ecstasy. I've known ecstasy with April. There were times when holding her I felt that I conquered her. Interesting word. It wasn't that I really conquered. That's not really true—that I won among all the suitors.

(The word "suitors" conjured up the image of a group of men competing for the hand of a fair maiden. It sounded very Lancelot-like to me, and I wanted to know more about what he meant. Very simply, I asked, "Were you a suitor?")

I was absolutely a suitor! I did everything . . . like, you know, daring things—that kind of idea. I was an acrobat, and I was starting to do some weight lifting and dance. I was always a fairly good dancer, and I remember now—it was dancing and singing. By the way, I was one of the best singers. . . . So we could almost sing songs to each other . . .

(He'd said enough. I wanted him to return to the feeling of ecstasy he had talked about. When he paused, I interjected, "You were saying that you knew ecstasy.")

I knew ecstasy in a relationship, and it was in the ecstasy that I was totally transported. I was so happy. When I thought it was me with April, and I would yearn for her, for more than a couple of months, I think it was, say, three years. And everything I was doing would be for making April proud of me.

You know, I welcome this opportunity because I haven't really

talked in these terms for a long time. . . . She'd be proud of
me. . . . I was—seeking to relive these moments of great glory,
great glory, great joy. And I . . . and I don't now. I've known
them in dreams. . . . I mean literally in dreams.

I asked Jack Able about his dreams, and I will tell you later
what he had to say. But first, I want to say a bit more about
Lancelots like Jack Able. These men are not in the man-
servant minister's business of worshiping "powerful, perfect" women. Nor are they in the man-servant educator's
business of transforming women who are "handicapped." In
order to give to women, Lancelots strut. They display their
plumage in competition with other men to be the most
alluring, arousing, exciting of the flock. That is the nature
of their *instrumental giving*. Lancelots believe that women
respond to that sort of behavior. Women choose winners.
They want "real" men with whom they can be "queen of the
prom" and feel proud and protected, while basking in the
Lancelots' glory.

Lancelots imagine that the power of their achievements
will **conquer** women. (Women have a button labeled
POWER. Push it and she's yours.) Captured and captivated
by a man's power, women will surrender themselves. A
powerful man can have it all. He can feel whole and completely wonderful. Consider Jack Able's dream:

Just vaguely, I remember . . . the physical nature of having so-
called wet dreams. But the wetness of the dreams as they occurred
was . . . yeah, there was a recurring one of flying and seeing
*suddenly this wonderful **creature**. And I fly right down to her*
and wrap my wings and arms around her. And rub my body, and
our bodies could melt into each other. And then I would have an

ejaculation. But it was . . . it was such a wonderful, incredibly good experience.

Lancelots dream about having extrahuman power. They can swoop down, capture, and absorb wonderful she-creatures. Taking women's libidinal bounty in this way is exhilarating for Lancelots, to the point where they reach orgasm. Dream pleasures are short-lived, however, and when Lancelots awaken to the sound of reality's alarm, they are destined to be disappointed.

Blaming

To the motto on the minister's crest, GAIN THROUGH GIV-ING, and the one on the educator's, GAIN THROUGH GUID-ING, add the Lancelot's: GAIN THROUGH PERFORMING.

Numero uno. A Lancelot's accomplishments are the means to an end that he will never reach. His money, trophies, muscles, cars, and fame are meant to dazzle women and make them swoon.

To Lancelots, the swooning is essential. Lancelots are driven. They cannot sit back, assured that their accomplishments have satisfied the elusive standards of the male competency cluster. For Lancelots, there is always another mountain to be climbed, more money to be made, or greater victories to be won. No matter what the arena of competition, Lancelots typically feel that sometime, someone out in the vague somewhere might—probably will—do better than they. Then they will not be *numero uno.*

Don't get me wrong. I think that striving to do well is a

terrific attribute, but only when the striving is enjoyed and produces a sense of contentment and satisfaction. When it is consciously or unconsciously motivated by a Lancelot's desire to dazzle women and make them swoon, there are terrible costs. Women aren't always dazzled by such behavior, and even when they are, they are never able to give Lancelots the libidinal bounty that they want. Lancelots have told me that they don't take kindly to women who fail to swoon and affirm them as *numero uno*.

Sol Edly, a man-servant Lancelot, explained to me that in his first marriage he was in the caretaker role. I asked Sol what happened then to cause him to say that about himself.

Well, first of all, my natural inclination is to be a very independent person—and decisive—and, you know, as my father taught me to do—stand on my own two feet and all this kind of stuff. So, in the initial contact my guess is that she [his first wife] *was attracted to me because of those qualities and I, no doubt, was attracted to her in a reciprocal sort of way for somewhat the same reasons. . . . She needed taking care of. And that fed into my own needs to be strong and powerful and so forth.*

(Unlike man-servant educators, Lancelots do not see women who attract them as diamonds in the rough with untapped potential. In Lancelots' eyes, the women need powerful men to *take care* of them. "It's a job for Lancelot!" The educator's fantasy of *guiding* women to a greater glory has little influence on Lancelots.

Naturally, I didn't say any of this to Sol Edly. What I did ask him, however, was what he got back for his caretaking efforts. There was a long pause, then he began speaking again.)

Well, a wife that was obedient, friendly, courteous, and kind.

82   HARVEY A. HORNSTEIN, PH.D.

[Sol laughed. When he finished, I asked, "Was she?] *Pretty much. Not that I, you know, was a tyrant or anything. . . . But there was—in a way I'm like that, but the decision, for example, after I finished school, where were we going to live. It was my decision. And there were choices, and she would have gone to any one of them. So that's what I mean about the obedient part. About the friendly, courteous, and kind—she's a decent woman. She was a good homemaker. Cared for the home—cared about the fact that I had three meals a day or whatever. That we had clean clothes and a clean house. All that kind of stuff. So I got a good caretaker of my nest.*

(What Sol Edy is telling us is that for a while, in small ways, she was dazzled by him, and it seemed to him that her bounty might be delivered. But that was not to be. Sol wanted what his wife couldn't give. What happened to Sol eventually happens to all Lancelots if they fail to develop insight into the syndrome: He experienced her "dazzlement" as diminished. He was no longer *numero uno*.)

*Motherhood seemed to be first and foremost for her. And, in fact, a major factor in **my** eventually separating—was that **motherhood** came so first, and that I became less and less first. To some extent she had found her **raison d'être**. . . . And so she pulled her life really into that and I began to play second fiddle more and more and more. . . . So that was another factor in my not feeling like I was getting as much in return.*

Lancelots may be saying, "Have your baby," or, less traditionally, "Have your career." But the covert, nonnegotiable contingency is, "Whatever you do, do it as an ***add-on***. Have your babies, career, or both, just as long as you *also* do all the nurturing, social, and domestic duty that befits me as *numero uno*."

The erotic Lancelot. What an image Lancelots have of women! Women are mindless and passive, programmed to take care of the nest and swoon at the sight of a Lancelot doing his thing. One of the most disturbing manifestations of this view is evident in Lancelots' sexual fantasies. Walk the streets of many of the world's major cities and you will eventually hear it expressed in several languages: "Hey baby, you know that you want it!" Lancelots expect women to respond sexually to the symbols of "manly" power just like children presented with their favorite flavor of lollipop.

In a mild way, the very first time Sol Edly met his former wife it was "Hey, baby, you know that you want it!" that attracted him to her.

We met in college and I, being older than she—I was actually a junior—when she was a freshman. How we actually met was all of us fraternity guys were scouting out all the women to look for our rush girls. . . . What impressed me about her in the first place, interestingly, on account of what I've been saying, besides being attractive, just personally and physically attractive, I didn't make the first move on her, in terms of asking her out or anything like that. What she did was to tell one of my fraternity brothers that she wanted to date me. And so she took the initiative to get word to me that I should ask her, which I did. So I liked that. I was impressed by that.

I call the Lancelot's erotic fantasy the *Seduction-Rape Fantasy.* Its basics are easy to describe; they were evident in Jack Able's dream. First, man seduces woman. (Sometimes that happens despite her considerable reluctance.) Second, the woman is so turned on that she all but rapes her irresistibly powerful seducer.

One man's story:

I was at this business conference—some Goddamned hotel someplace—I—that doesn't matter—she—this woman—I saw her—she was, I don't know fifty, fifty-two, but a young body. I thought—I was sitting, resting on a lounge on the terrace, minding my own beeswax, feeling pretty high and mighty about my presentation and found myself thinking that she had kind of looked at me. That set it off. I'm well built—lifted weights, exercise, you know—I thought that maybe she hadn't been with a young guy. She'd like to feel some muscle. Women can be like that. You know, young guys do it better.

(He laughed and waved the index and middle fingers of his two hands in the air, indicating that there were quotation marks around his last sentence, qualifying it as a joke. Without disputing or endorsing his finger-wagging qualifiers, I encouraged him to continue his fantasy.)

She'd be talking with me maybe in the bar, later. Then I'd go back—walk with her to her room. There's music—the radio or whatever—we'd—there's dancing. Then she—it's late and she says, "Good night"—but I can tell she wants—she's bothered. I don't say anything—just sort of not let go. She touches me, here [on his chest and shoulder], I don't know, maybe, saying no—you know, like, "Go but don't go." She's getting turned on. I'm gripping her and then—I don't know—she's all over me—really wanting it—out of sight.

Several Lancelot-style man-servants told me about special sexual experiences and erotic fantasies in which women "did it all." Lancelots seem to enjoy times when their roles and women's are reversed, with women becoming the powerful performers and Lancelots the recipients of their performance. I suppose that it's "out of sight" because Lancelots wouldn't want anyone to see them being so obviously passive and dependent, which, underneath the macho exterior, may be how they actually feel.

Lancelot's Seduction-Rape Fantasy reveals what ultimately produces tragedy for him as well as for the women in his life: "Hey baby, you know that you want it!" is a perniciously false claim. "Baby" is an adult woman and frequently, if not always, what she wants is a partner with whom she can share, not a performer who tries to subordinate her through intimidating displays of power.

Oppression

Jack Able spent much of his life performing for women.

Yeah, O.K., now coming back to the nature of me making commitments. . . . There are other women that I came close to marrying. . . . Quite a few—three or four come quickly to mind. . . . All, by the way, exceptionally beautiful women. . . . I didn't feel as if I could achieve. I've achieved this by now—by maturity— there's always a dream . . . that the only kind of man that these goddesses—just to coin a phrase, it's easier. I have to merit their respect and love. . . . And at various points in my life I wasn't in a place to merit that respect. And down deep I always felt about myself—I'm obviously telling you things very deeply personal that you must get from all men—about myself—there were insecurities that were unnamed. One is, for instance, keeping up with my brother. My brother looked like he was setting the world on fire. Very deeply self-confident . . . my brother was the hare of the family, I was sort of the tortoise. And it was what I thought about myself. I was very, very insecure as a kid. I felt it very hard to assert myself. Little did I realize as I got into the outside world that everyone found me very different than I found myself. They found I was quite assertive, "forceful," they'd say. And I used to turn to look over my shoulder. "Who's that, me?" Was it my brother behind me? It was very true. And all that relates to the relationship with women.

(Jack Able then explained how all that related to his relationships with women. He began by telling me how he felt when his brother came back from Korea, a war hero.)

He was attractive to women. And when he came back, I remember all those medals and ribbons and—uh—was I worthy? That goes back now to link to the women—to the relationship to females. . . . I had to find my manhood. That was a very important time.

Man-servant syndrome fools Lancelots into seeking, in a woman's response to their performance, affirmative answers to questions that they have about their manhood. But if a man's sense of manhood is infected by feelings of "frogness," then there is nothing permanent that a woman can do to kiss those feelings away.

Never recognizing that they want what women cannot give, Lancelots become angry with women for being so "cold," "rejecting," and "unloving" (despite Lancelots' best efforts), and also disappointed in themselves for what appears to them as substandard performance. Finally, they lash out. In a desperate effort they bully women into behaving as if they were powerless. Then, for a little while, Lancelots can feel powerful. The point is illustrated by what Alex Teufel told me.

*   *   *

I'd make her cry—easily. She'd cry easily. Get angry—sometimes they bawl like hell. [I noted that he went from the pronoun "she," to "they," suggesting that what he was saying didn't apply to his behavior in just one relationship.] *I wouldn't call, after promising, you know, and then say, "Don't control me"—or I'd refuse to go out when we were expected. There was a date or something. You know, dumb things but—it was dumb— but it made her cry.*

("When might you do these things?")

I dunno.

(Being persistent, I asked, "Is there one time that stands out?")

Yeah. When I got news about . . . [He mentioned a promotion.] *We celebrated—or tried to.*

("Tried to?")

Yeah. It bombed. She—you know—ahh—you work your ass off, take care of it all, make it: good money, good life—so she can be proud—do the suburban, country-club bit, but there's nothing, like it's nothing. She was a cold bitch.

Alex Teufel's wife, interviewed on a separate occasion, said: *My God. He was always puffed up, as if it were enough for a body just to be with King Whatever. Ooooo! It upsets me just to think of it. Anyway, I don't know why, but that night I was just filled right up to here* [she slashed her hand across her throat in the approximate position of her Adam's apple]. *I was pleased, believe me, very pleased, but I wanted to tell him about my day as well. I'm not sure that he ever heard about me, in all the years, you know. No—I'm sure that he never did. He was that absorbed in himself.*

Answering my inquiry about how he wanted her to respond, he said, *Well, hell, it's a major accomplishment. At least at that time in our lives. You know—how a woman's supposed to respond. I dunno. It's a big thing. I can't—really—not gratitude—something. Pleasure—some real joy—it seems so evident that it's hard. . . .*

(Later, when I told him about man-servant syndrome and men's fantasies about what women can give, he said sadly, "Where were you when I needed you?" When I learned how this episode unfolded, I too wished that I had been there earlier.)

I felt down, really down. I guess I took it out on her. Yeah. That was . . . it was a bad one.

("A bad one?")

I was physical. It became physical.

His wife said: *He was actually violent. There had been other episodes, but never quite so . . . I was frightened. But, by golly, this time I didn't take it. Good-bye Charlie. Honestly, I don't think that he believed I could do it. I don't think I quite believed it. Good-bye Charlie.*

BRINGING UP
MAN-SERVANT

Time:	July 1989—Twilight
Setting:	Parents' night at summer camp. Logs blaze in a stone fireplace located at the center of a natural woodland amphitheater. Hemlocks, green and sweet-smelling, the theater's living wall, are a dramatic backdrop for the children's performances.
Observation:	After each trio of senior and junior counselor and counselor-in-training introduces itself and its choice of a name (the Bopping Bats or Hip Hamsters), each camper is invited to tell the parents who he or she is. The girls do so, quietly, gently, and at times, barely audibly. Their voices blend with nature's chorus of birds, crickets, and rustling branches. Then it is the boys' turn! Their screams assault the stillness as each boy strives to shout his name

louder than all the boys who went before him. After six-year-old Donald's incredible scream causes some in the audience to wince, his mother, who is sitting on a log behind me, says, to no one in particular, "That's my little man."

Time: June 1989—Late afternoon
Setting: An elementary school class picnic in Manhattan's Central Park
Observation: While parents are cleaning up the picnic's refuse, a group of girls has formed a chorus line. The girls are rehearsing a routine, which they plan to present to their parents. Another group of girls is skipping rope. A few girls are being chased around trees by boys, who growl loudly while curling their fingers into claws. Some other girls and boys are in the trees around which the chase is occurring. The boys, perched on the highest branches, challenge and belittle one another and the girls for being either poor climbers or lacking in daring. One group of boys is not playing with any girls. With lots of shouting and insult-filled disagreement about skill, strategy, rules, tags, and fair balls, this group is playing baseball. After one such dispute, a father talks in hushed tones to his son, who lost the argument about a tag at first base. I overhear the father say, "You're just not trying hard enough."

Time: Autumn 1988
Setting: A playground in suburban New Jersey
Observation: A mother flips the pages of a magazine while
               keeping watch as her two children play "para-
               troop." The boy appears to be about five years
               of age and the girl perhaps two or three years
               older. Arms yoked across each other's shoul-
               ders, they are leaping in unison. On the eigh-
               teenth jump, there is a communications
               failure and tragedy strikes. Their synchronic-
               ity is lost, and they tumble to the ground in
               a jumble, striking elbows, knees, and heads.
               There is no blood, but both are crying. Mom
               bounds to her kids. Her right arm goes
               around Jacqueline, who buries her face on
               Mom's shoulder. There are pats for Jacque-
               line. Mom's left hand is on Jimmy's right
               shoulder. She shakes him a bit. Speaking over
               the children's tearful moans, Mom advises,
               "Be a big boy, Jimmy. Big boys don't cry."

Turning Princes into Frogs

Jack and the other boys I observed were learning about
the male competency cluster: Males are supposed to be
winners, in charge, independent, strong, courageous, self-
reliant, and decisive. They provide and protect, are generally noisy, sometimes naughty, but not often emotional.

The experiences of these boys are illustrative of conclu-
sions based on evidence collected from thousands of children, using rigorous research procedures. This evidence
shows that:

- Parents prize boys' aggressiveness, calling it "bold" and "dynamic," describing their aggressive sons with such fond words as "bombshell." But when parents see the very same behavior from their daughters, they say that it is being caused by "anxiety" and "confusion." It is something in need of fixing.
- Mothers, as well as fathers, pressure boys more than girls to achieve.
- In contrast to infant girls' experiences, the more infant boys cry, the *less* their moms are nurturant. The message is: "Young man, you need to be self-reliant and tough." Jimmy of suburban New Jersey learned that crying begot barely veiled criticism of his manliness, rather than the comforting pats offered to sister Jacqueline.
- Little girls are more emotional than little boys.

Some critics of this last conclusion about boys' lack of emotional expression have pointed out that most investigations of male-female emotions have used self-report, paper-and-pencil measures. You know the kind: On a continuum of one to ten, "How often do you cry (or feel anxious, or fearful)?" or, "How do you respond when . . . ?" With this kind of evidence, these critics argue, it is entirely possible that the differences between males and females occur because males are less willing than females to report these sorts of reactions; and if behavior was actually directly observed, no differences between the sexes would appear.

From the perspective of man-servant syndrome, it really doesn't matter very much whether the self-reports are accurate accounts of experience or are simply reflections of gender differences in reluctance or willingness to admit being emotional. Either way, the evidence shows just how enslaved men are: In their actual experience, self-presentation, or both, men are compelled to fulfill the stereotype embodied in the male competence cluster.

The problem for little boys is that they *do* cry. They are also sometimes afraid of climbing trees' highest boughs, and some are not always their group's most able athletes. On occasion, their little vocal cords simply will not permit them to scream louder than all the other boys. Fairy tales, movies, and television may tempt them into trying to become Prince Charming–type rescuers who confront demons and dragons of every variety, but when they are alone, and have to walk down a dark corridor or by a partly opened closet door, little boys can feel more intimidated than bold.

When their parents are injured or become ill, it frightens little boys. Large bullies scare them, and so do the shouts of angry teachers. The problem for little boys is that they *do cry* and, normally, their lives are filled with thoughts, feelings, and behaviors that fall short of the male competency cluster's elusive, idealized standards. Little boys are painfully aware of these "failings" and, as long as they believe that the cluster's standards are really something to aspire to, the result is self-doubt.

A conversation with adults or friends could help them. Someone might just tell them how unrealistic their aspirations are. But it's hard for boys to tell people about their feelings. Their doubts must be kept hidden because insecurity, uncertainty, anxiety, and fear violate the male competency cluster requirement that a man be dauntless.

How ironic, and how like a metaphor for fairy tales this whole tragic sequence is: Expectations that **boy** will be superior—a Prince Charming—imposes standards that cannot possibly be met. **Boy** is set up for an unavoidable fall.

When it occurs, it is as if he committed some transgression. He feels inadequate and substandard, more the frog than the prince.

Maurice Mandar (Man-Servant Syndrome, Style: Educator) explained to me why he behaved as he did toward his first wife:

Now, this had a lot to do with my mother, who was someone who came from that kind of background . . . who didn't get past high school but had . . . ambitions to go to college. Ambitions, I think . . . to be an engineer. She married a man who went to . . . two years of college after he began working . . . whom she thought of as really not quite at her intellectual level. And there was a whole vicarious thing that she had in the process of my schooling—much more involved and invested than I would have liked to have had. She wanted to know everything about what we were doing, and particularly by the time I got to high school, and there were subjects like calculus, which she hadn't had, and she wanted to study calculus with me.

(The impression that Mom did not get all that she needed from Dad was common among the men I interviewed. Some spoke of Mom's neediness as something that they once believed in, but now doubted; others believed that their mothers were still needy at the time of the interview.

Maurice experienced his mom as turning to him to replace what was missing. I asked him about this, suggesting that he had become her teacher.)

I think—in some ways. It was not completely one-sided. I was a kid and I needed help sometimes. That's what I got in return. . . . I went to a high school that was very challenging, from a grammar school that was not at all challenging. . . . I was panicked. I had never had to work like that and, you know, I got support. I got soothed and encouraged, and told that I could do it. That was very helpful.

*But once I found my stride and I knew that I could really shine in the environment, all I had to do was shift gears—then it became very much a feeling that I was taking **her** on trips into the big world. . . . I was sort of a Marco Polo coming back to the Venice of my family.*

(He then qualified his statement: "Venice" was his mom, not the whole family.)

. . . No one else really gave a damn about very much. I mean they were glad I was having a good time, but that was really about it. But for her, it was, "Let's hear all about it!"

(Now I became more explicit, saying that it sounded as if she was asking him to fulfill needs that were not being fulfilled elsewhere.)

Right! I mean, one of the most frustrating experiences I can remember, and still has echoes today [was when] I would be playing on the floor, in the kitchen, as a preschooler, and my mother would bring in the ironing board, and set it up . . . and then she would talk to me.

(I commented again about the demands that she was placing on him. He responded with a description of how they felt to him.)

They were scary. They were scary, but at the same time the thought that I might be able to—I was lionized, particularly by my mother for being smart and clever and sensitive and—you know—that was pretty heady stuff. . . . What it creates is a sense of always being in danger of screwing up royally.

I guess when a potential prince violates the cluster's "regal" standards because he behaves as if he were a gawky frog, it qualifies as a case of "screwing up royally."

Dad Was a Frog Too

Sol Edly (Man-Servant Syndrome, Style: Lancelot) spoke about his parents:

I never saw her as really happy. I saw her as complaining about his always having to have his way, and, uh, making decisions. . . . She never did anything to counter it or to actually deal with it other than just accept it and complain about it. . . . Actually, way later in life . . . after I was grown and away from home, she would talk even more openly to us children, as adults, about his faults. In terms of having to have his way and all this kind of stuff. She would always attribute it to the fact that he . . . was babied all of his life and so he had to have his way.

(At this point, I urged Sol to tell me more about his mother. He started by reminding me that his dad had died.)

She's been doing fine on her own . . . lives by herself and makes it. . . . She could have done that a long time ago and why didn't she? It's extremely difficult to know . . . later in life what my mother would do—she would begin to kind of . . . rebel against him and not do some things that he would want to do. . . . And when I would go home, and Dad and I would be together, then he would talk to me about her. [Sol laughed.] So, you know, I was in a counselor role as a son. It was amazing. . . . But what kind of blew me away in terms of how my own life is—I don't mean to overstate this—but, how in a lot of ways I replicate that whole process.

Men often replicate their dad's behavior. They do so even when (or perhaps *especially* when) they disapprove of it. One reason that they replicate Dad's behavior is because for little boys, Dad is a prominent and sometimes solitary example of how men behave toward women.

Dads are men too. In their dealings with women, they control, criticize, and instruct. They absorb themselves in making money, the job, their parents, sports, hobbies, TV, and other women. Rather than being *with* Mom, they *do for, to,* and *in front of* her. So if Dad suffers man-servant syndrome, then its symptoms are there for his son to learn.

A second, less apparent way in which dads contribute to the development of the man-servant syndrome in their sons arises from the neediness that sons believe dads have inflicted on their moms. A son sees Mom shouldering burdens that drain her energy and time, restricting his access to her emotional bounty. Are moms and dads causing their sons to have this view of what's happening to Mom? Sometimes yes: Travail in a marriage may result in Mom's private desperation or public announcement of her neediness. At other times, however, parents are not so obviously responsible for their sons' view of Mom's world. Sometimes sons simply interpret the ordinary in extraordinary ways. It permits them to feel a bit bigger and more important if they, not Dad, are responsible for mending Mom's (imagined) neediness.

Thus, Mom may simply be a vehicle for her son's self-serving fantasies about what her world is like. Whatever the cause, the end result is that her *son's* internal experience convinces him that **Mom's deprivation deprives him** and something must be done. For little boys the solution is as clear as it is futile: If I can become to her what *he* is not, then she will be free of her burdens and able to give me what she possesses in return for what I have given her.

Jack Able (Man-Servant, Style: Lancelot) speaks:

ABOUT DAD: . . . *My father was always a strong masculine image from the viewpoint of being too macho. My mother was* *afraid of him to some extent. . . . My father played a very, very male role orientation in the traditional way—macho. I mean, he would raise his voice and I would have to keep quiet. . . . Very hard to talk back to my father. He was the authority. He was frightening.*

ABOUT MOM: *There were dreams that were created through Mom—whether they were false dreams or unfalse dreams. I mean, there was an aura of where she came from, and her dreams and the frustrations, that she couldn't realize her dreams in her lifetime. She could not. She could not.*

She did as a young child, but when she came into maturity, she went and married and, uh, I'll be frank . . . a mismarriage, where my mother really married down in terms of marrying a poorer man, a less educated man: my father. . . . She could not grow through that relationship, so I guess . . . she tried to grow through the children—the sons.

(On Saturday mornings, when her husband was away, she and her sons would sit together in bed and have conversations. During these conversations, her sons learned about both her dreams and frustrations.)

We came from a very strong upper class on my mother's side. My father's [family] was much more humble. . . . My mother's side were very powerful, very rich people.

(Jack told me there was a town that bears his mother's family's name.)

They were like feudal lords. We're talking about hundreds of years . . . we had ambassadors. . . . It sounds like a snob thing, but it's not. The important thing is that whatever people have . . . they can tie to when things are bad for them—it is important that they hold onto.

. . . Now, coming back to man-woman relationships, this does

*somehow interrelate to all this in a way. Because of the importance
of my mother it became a focal point for my brother and I in terms
of our dreams.*

John Noblework (Man-Servant, Style: Minister) speaks of
his family:

*I grew up in a single parent family. Just my mother and four
kids. . . . I never lived with my father at all . . . divorce. . . .
I know him. I visited him . . . when I was eighteen, going off to
the military, after I graduated from high school, and then I didn't
see him again until—for maybe ten or fifteen years. And then I was
married, and brought my [child] to see him. We met that one time
and then he died about four months later, so it never really got to
the healing, and a working relationship.*

(I asked him about how it was for him and his mom in a
single parent situation.)

*She was a brick. I mean really. She worked all of the time. You
know, she tried to guide us and she was active in the community.
She was active in the church. She was amazing. How she made it,
I don't know.*

(Man-servants often speak about their mothers in admir-
ing terms despite the accompanying belief that they were
awfully demanding and unsatisfied with their lot in life.
The dissonant quality of these thoughts always reminds me
of one aspect of animal-groom fairy tales such as "The Frog
Prince." In these stories, the transformation of the prince
into an animal is typically caused by an older female sor-
ceress or witch who remains unpunished for committing
this magical mutation. Also the stories typically leave ob-
scure the reasons for her deed, although it is hard to escape
the implication that she did it because—in her eyes—the
prince committed some transgression. With these thoughts

in mind, I asked John, "How did you respond to that hard work—that commitment?" His answer reveals the maternal deprivation that he felt.)

*Well, I guess early in my life I didn't appreciate how driven she was. I thought she was a harsh disciplinarian and that **everything that she did was calculated around managing the family, and money, and this kind of thing.** . . . She always had to get us to help out in the work and to do things all the time. Even at a very early age, I had to help out. I sold papers when I was four or five. Then . . . I started working in grocery stores—working weekends and stuff. From the time I was about nine or ten, I more or less bought my own clothes. . . . I paid for my own lunches and all that. She very rarely had to give me any money. In fact, I supported her when I was in the military.*

. . . When I was in the military, I decided that what I wanted to do was go to college, so that I needed to save a lot of money. . . . So I took out savings bonds and I put them in my name and in my mother's name. I sent them home. . . . It may have been before I got out of service, or maybe it was after, I found out that I didn't have any of the savings bonds that I was saving for my college education. . . . So I got out basically broke.

("She used the money? She cashed the bonds?")

She needed it so I couldn't get upset. I think I wanted to get upset.

("But it was hard?")

Yeah. It was hard to get upset.

John Noblework, Jack Able, Sol Edly, and Maurice Mandar are from different generations. They have different ethnic and religious backgrounds. But there is at least one thing they do have in common: All four have experienced man-servant syndrome. Each of them has heard his mother whisper her need and, in response, each has acted as if he believed she wanted him to replace what was missing in her life. With a little boy's superficial understanding of what Mom needed from Dad, John, Jack, Sol, and Maurice tried to fill the gap.

The problem is that little boys have an immature understanding of how romantic partnerships are nourished by respect, encouragement, support, honor, and trust. What boy understands, instead, is that Mom's deprivation (and therefore his own as well) will be taken care of if he is a good boy who provides for her (the minister who *does for*), a smart boy who guides her (the educator who *does to*), or a powerful boy who takes care and protects her (the Lancelot who *does in front of*).

This distorted understanding of the subtle world of male-female relationships influences a boy's efforts and also dooms them. What Mom lacks because of Dad (if in reality she lacks anything at all) boy cannot provide. Despite his efforts she will remain discontented. Instead of providing the impossible, magical relief that he fantasizes about, boy's every effort is bound to fail. "I was never able to make her happy. She never seemed satisfied." The end is the beginning: Each of his efforts leaves him feeling more gawky, repulsive, and in need of women's cleansing bounty.

Independently Dependent

Once the circle is closed in this way it marks the start of a lifelong struggle between independence and dependence. The boy believes that he is supposed to become a man who is independent, self-reliant, and strong, a smart doer and shaker who can take care of women, but he does not feel that way. There is self-doubt. Mom's miseries continue. His efforts have not produced the relieving embrace that he fantasizes Mom can provide. He has been unable to take care of her. He cries. Worse, sometimes he feels as if he would like someone to take care of him.

Man-servant syndrome seems as if it might be a solution by falsely promising the impossible: A man can be independently dependent. How? If he maintains the illusion of superiority by taking care of women while actually being a supplicant who is serving in order to receive the affirming bounty that he imagines women possess. The master is servant, and the servant, master.

In this way, man-servant syndrome provides temporary relief of painful symptoms while the problem festers. The syndrome is a tranquilizer that dulls the stress. But this psychological cover-up does not resolve the underlying conflict between seemingly contradictory, irreconcilable desires for independence and dependence. As boy grows to man, the emotional tug-of-war inside him grows as well until it becomes a major obstacle to forming satisfying, committed relationships with women.

Consider Willy Bethair's experiences. He began our conversation by telling me about a recurring fantasy that he has about women.

. . . The fantasy revolves around someone in need, and my being around to help out. . . . When I sort of get out of the fantasy, I realize I really don't want to take care of anyone for any long length of time. And, obviously, if I'm going to be a decent person and I agree to take care of someone, I am almost compelled, ethically, to take care of them until someone else takes care. . . . So,

if I begin a relationship taking care of them, rescuing them, then I'm stuck with them. So, I realize that in my fantasy, and I say that's enough of that. I don't need it . . . I don't want to take care of someone who is going to give you trouble—right? . . . I sort of choose a fantasy in which, through no fault of my person, they have been left to drift without resources, and I'm a rescuer. I pick them up . . .

Curiously enough, now that I'm reflecting on it, each time I have **actually** *had a woman who was dependent upon me, I did not want dependency. Whereas I was willing to rescue them, I was not willing to take care of them in the dependent kind of relationship. And now that I'm focusing on it, I remember being really annoyed that there was a* quid pro quo *for this. . . . I wasn't getting back what I was putting into it, right? [And] I didn't want what was given back; so I was becoming annoyed with getting stuck with a dependent relationship.*

(Later, I pointed out to Willy that women who needed rescuing might be prone to being more dependent than those who were not in need of rescuing. He agreed that might be the case, so I asked him why then did he bother forming relationships with women who were more likely to present a problem with which he did not want to contend? He was unexpectedly blunt. Such women are "submissive," he said.)

. . . That makes me more powerful; the more people I can rescue the more powerful [I am].

(When Willy Bethair told me about his childhood, it was easy to see evidence of familiar patterns nurturing the development of man-servant syndrome in him.)

I grew up in Pittsburgh; I was born in Atlanta. . . . Both [parents] finished high school. Both were menial laborers. . . . I was much closer to Mother—yeah, much closer to Mother—so much so that in later years—well, let me tell you the story: My mother was very supportive and always encouraging. . . . I always felt protective of Mother because I felt her to be vulnerable. **She had a way of moaning about her fate which was distressing at times.** *We were very poor, and my father, while he is a very responsible man* [he] *is also, in a word, "stingy.". . . Consequently, I perceive Mother as trying to get things done and manage things. Dad was always reluctant to dispense with the funds, to make things happen. He was a hard worker—very responsible—very dedicated, but very, very tight.* **So, I think of Mother always complaining about the struggle she was trying to make it with Dad.** *So, the rescuing began very early: rescuing Mother! . . . My brother was relatively irresponsible. He was no help at all. That left me to take care of things; helping my mother out when neither my dad nor my brother would do so.*

(Willy told me that he went to college. His brother, at seventeen, left home to join the military, and his father philandered.)

But their final break came in my last semester . . . after twenty-five years, which devastated Mother. . . . She had given Dad such a hard time most of the times I can remember them being together—always complaining about his behavior, whatever, and how he didn't help, and didn't support, and didn't tah de, tah de, tah de, da! So it was really a surprise to me when he finally left the house [that] *she was devastated.*

She didn't know how she was going to make it. How she was going to support herself, etc. As a second lieutenant, making two hundred and seventy-five dollars a month, I gave her one hundred and seventy-five dollars a month to take care of herself. So, that pattern . . .

*   *   *

Willy Bethair never finished the sentence. He didn't need to. We both knew that the "pattern" of his youth became the pattern of his early adulthood, and would be the pattern of relationships with women well into his middle adult years.

As a little boy, Willy heard the same whispers that John, Jack, Maurice, Sol, Steven, and all other men who experience man-servant syndrome hear: "I need you to be my little man." Dad has done things; Mom is needy. Did she actually say it? It makes no difference. **Boy** hears that simple plea, or one of its many variations, and regardless of whether the request is real or imagined, if it goes unchallenged, it is a scream of "*Open Sesame!*" in front of gates leading to the dark cavern of man-servant syndrome.

MAN-SERVANT
MEETS MS.

Work is "genderfied." Nearly everywhere in this world there is a stereotypical view of what is men's work and what is women's. Anthropological studies produce very few examples of societies where men and women have the same occupational roles; and in those few instances where the genders' daily vocational toils overlap, it is the men who generally occupy the prestigious positions, controlling access to society's treasured icons.

Sigmund Freud lent an unwitting hand to work "genderfication" when he wrote that women represent the interests of the family and sexual life, but the work of civilization is men's business.

Freud's claim, now sixty years old, seems contrary to current employment trends as well as labor-pool projections, which reveal that during the next decade, more than two thirds of all married women will be working. Women who might appear to represent only "the interests of the family and sexual life" will be the exceptions. These developments might cause some folks to applaud the liberalization of modern society and discount the Austrian gentleman's claim as if it were some quaintly outdated product of a mind shaped by a traditional, nineteenth-century Victorian society.

In their rush to write an epitaph for work genderfication, however, these folks miss a crucial point: Work genderfication's most profound consequences are reflected in men's treatment of working women, not in any statistics on the percentage of women who work. And on this point, the comments by men and women I interviewed support rather consistent findings from behavioral science research showing that, often without any awareness at all, men maintain work genderfication by treating Ms. Employee as if she were "out-of-place, off her turf, and doing things not in keeping with her natural skills and abilities as a woman."

Joe Layudar, a tall good-looking man in his late forties, has national prominence in his profession. His job brings him into contact with a number of publicly and privately funded organizations committed to improving the general welfare of less fortunate citizens. He works with many women. One of them is Terri, who he introduced into our conversation by describing some of the ways in which his perception of her work-related ability was at odds with his behavior toward her.

[Terri] . . . *is a very competent person in our organization* . . . [who has] *inherited the chair of a committee that's to* [advise on certain personnel policy]. *Now, she is a tough woman, who is very confident . . . and she can handle herself. There is a way in which her tough management of the committee makes me feel that it comes at a higher expense for her than it ought. I find that I get much more coordinated to what she's trying to accomplish . . . than I think I would if it were a man. I try to help her to do the business. It's implicitly clear that between the two of us that's going on.*

(On the surface this might seem like nothing more than a decent effort to help a woman colleague, but, as you will learn, Joe Layudar's motives in helping this woman involve more than simple collegial compassion. What he is getting from this "helping" effort, and what he is signaling to Terri, provide supporting evidence of both work genderfication and man-servant syndrome.)

There was a situation last week where she had to take [an executive] on. She'd gone farther out than I thought was necessary. I found myself taking a very extreme position—being tougher than I really felt was necessary with [the executive]. I was doing it because I was being supportive to her, and she was out there, and I felt like "this role comes at a very high price for her," and she does it nobly, and she really needs help.

*When I reflected on it afterwards, I wondered how much of that had to do with man-woman, because somehow even though she was a very able woman, being the only one in the room, and taking on something so tough—**I realized that much of my empathy with her situation came out of a fantasy about the fact that that's more difficult for her.***

(I asked Joe to tell me more about what he imagined went into making this sort of situation more difficult for Terri.)

I haven't a good sense of why it's more difficult for her. There are lots of women in our organization—so it's a fairly balanced thing. But there are not very many at her level. . . . I don't know. It's really unscrutinized. . . . It feels to me like it's hard for her. She

*is straining at the role. The role she is going to do well no matter
what the cost. My feeling about it is that the cost is hard.*

("How do you feel when you come to her aid?")

I feel good. It feels noble.

(Hearing the possible influence of man-servant syndrome
in admitting that by helping this "needy" woman, Joe gains
nobility, I asked him to describe how his behavior made
him feel noble.)

*My feeling is that she needs more help. . . . My help makes the
situation better. And, because I care about her, I do that. I really
don't have anything except feelings that lead me to conclude it has
to do with man-woman. That's the first thing that came into my
mind and I know that was the connection because that's the feeling
I have. . . . I keep saying that she's a very competent woman, and
she really can take care of herself, but somehow it seems to me that
the effective-affective use of this role comes at a very high price for
her. . . . I don't know that it's the temporary loss of her stereotypic
femininity or whatever, but it's just the—it's hard to push these
guys around. I know it is.*

("So, if you help, it relieves her burden?")

*Well, absolutely! It does two things: It says that she's not being
excessive—I think she fears that she doesn't have a good way to
read whether she's overplaying the role because she feels the strain of
the role so much, or that she's handling it properly. And it also
allows her time to pull back and look at it.*

(I drew him back to the "noble" part by asking, "You
feel ennobled by doing that?")

*Absolutely! To such a degree that I probably take a lot more
extreme positions around her issues than I would otherwise.*

(He hesitated. "It pushes you to be more extreme?" I
prompted.)

Not categorically different . . . only in degree. Like, it's not *necessary to be out as far as she is, but because she's there she **needs** me to be there with her. I'll be there with her.*

(Again a hesitation, and I encouraged him to go on.)

I was raised before anybody invented the women's movement. I was raised in a family where values around gesture and deed were really very clear. . . . When I was in high school, there was no question we would get out of the car and rip around to the other side and open the door for our date. And those became reflexes and also the attitudes and assumptions . . . about women. After the women's movement it's hard to know how to act because my reflex is always to open the door . . . always to be sort of helpful.

(Helping co-workers is a fine thing to do. But as was the case with many of the other men with whom I spoke, Joe Layudar was not just being helpful—and he had the insight to suspect this. Imbedded in his helpfulness was a message: Working women need help because their natural endowment handicaps their performance on the job. It's self-serving for men with the syndrome to make this assumption. It concludes that because work is alien to women, in order to survive, they need men's help. This logic provides an apparently noble justification for men co-workers to *do for, to,* and *in front of* women. Joe was more conscious of these dynamics than many of the other men with whom I spoke, but even he was being maneuvered by their power.)

There were very clear prescriptions. And I still get pleasure out of interacting with women who enjoy that [men helping] *and are not ambivalent about it. That's also an interesting process. I think implicitly, as you get to know someone, there's partly a . . . quality of flirtation in it. There's a quality of explicitly negotiating expectations, but I enjoy the relationships with women that begin to evolve in the direction of their communicating pleasure.*

("Pleasure, at what?")

In my being supportive. In my facilitating making decisions. In my—that whole traditional role stuff.

("How do you see yourself when you're experiencing that sort of pleasure?")

That I'm a good man. That I'm the kind of man I should be and I'm appreciated for it. . . . And it feels like there are appropriate niches, and they work for us.

And that is amusing to me as I think about it now. Due to the fact that I'm also a gay man and in that context don't play out a whole set of role prescriptions for standard American males.

Society plants the roots of man-servant syndrome deep into a man's being. Resistant to easy removal, they eventually form a symbiotic relationship with genderfication of work. The resultant thinking goes like this: Work, having to do with the material, not the emotional world, is man's "natural" domain. It is a private preserve where men hope that they can gather what is necessary to provide for, guide, and dazzle women. But if women are somehow able to enter this domain and *do* for themselves, then men will lose a fundamental means of accumulating what they need in order to win women's bounty.

A cartoon in an October 1989 issue of *The New Yorker* magazine tells us why men fear that this loss will occur. It shows two yuppie-type men sitting on either side of a small round table in a café. They look bereft. The caption explains why: One of them is lamenting, "She's her own man."

Thus, Ms. Employee, autonomous, competent, breadwinner, presents a problem for many men. If she is qualified to do "his" work, and becomes "her own man," then how is a man to become a **man**? How will he gather the evidence that he needs in order to persuade a woman to surrender her bounty and affirm his identity?

Take note: Man-servant's doubts about his identity are not erased by success at work. Many of the men with whom I spoke were wealthy, prestigious, and physically powerful, but still felt frustrated, unfulfilled, and uncertain of themselves as men. Despite the reality of their "manly" successes, they were searching for "the right woman," believing that *she* would give them the peace of mind that they craved.

For these men, and many others like them, work is only a means of acquiring evidence.

In the end, women, not men, judge the worthiness of their work and, by implication, their worthiness as men. Men are reduced to hoping that women will respond to their successes at work by offering their special, affirming bounty. This bounty is the fantastic, fantasized reward they imagine will finally eradicate the "frogness" within them and provide "forever after" comfort and conviction in their masculinity.

But if women work, and as a consequence acquire power, control, and possession of society's prized resources, man-servants are bound to feel bereft. They have lost a means of winning women's affirming libidinal bounty. Women's advances in the work world threaten to destroy man-servants' means of acquiring identity. Now, it's a matter of self-preservation. **Women's access must be blocked.**

Dancing with Amazons

Stanley Ped, an unmarried man working as a salesperson in a shoe store, told me about the end of a torrid love affair that had occurred ten years earlier, when he was twenty-eight years old. He and the woman, whom he'd met at a disco, were together almost three years when she finished her MBA and accepted a position in banking. Her income vaulted upward, surpassing his by tens of thousands of dollars. He complained to me about how her new work life altered their relationship:

She was never there anymore. Between the office and trips—the West Coast, Chicago, you know. And the talking; always about her damned job.

It was something—I didn't really think about it this way before, but now that we're speaking about it—it's really clear. Like, she canceled my ticket. Like a dance ticket. I had a ticket to dance with a woman and she ends up being kind of an amazon. **You don't dance with an amazon.** *You find a woman who wants you to safely guide her across the dance floor, making her feel graceful and feminine-like—and you know, you feel good that way.*

One Sunday morning, very nearly on the first anniversary of her new job, Stanley Ped packed his bags and, by that afternoon, moved in with another woman with whom he had been having an affair for about one month. She was a college dropout who worked in the shoe store as a clerk.

Stanley's response to the first woman, the one he called an "amazon," caught the attention of investigators trying to explain women's self-limiting behavior in the workplace. Their data suggest that one of the reasons that women fail to achieve their potential in domains that are stereotypically masculine is that they fear the consequences of surpassing current and future male partners: A woman who pulls ahead blocks their route to masculinity, causing them to perceive that her femininity has been compromised.

In time, men like Stanley Ped confirm women's fear by ending their relationships with them. What is often confusing to women is that before the final good-bye, men's messages frequently contain what appears to be pleasure over women's success in the work field, but no indication of other thoughts.

There is evidence from Stanley Ped, as well as from the other men and women I interviewed, that for some men, despite the threat of successful working women, there are occasions when these women hold particular allure. Somehow their potency in a "man's world" makes their bounty seem that much greater. In addition, a man touched by the syndrome is inclined to think that, "If I can provide for or protect **such a** woman, then I will prove myself to be a special man."

Now I've got to tell you that what I said before—there's a contradiction.

("What kind of contradiction?")

I was sort of really turned on at first by [he mentioned the first woman's name] *when she finished her degree and got the job. It was definitely a kind of sexual thing. Definitely. I'd even say that for a while our sex life got more exciting.*

("How do you explain that?")

I don't know. She looked fantastic. But it was this kind of challenge. Here is this great-looking woman—everybody, like, admires her—she is really something special at [the banking house] *and, I suppose, it's that she's giving herself to me. It didn't feel like that after a while, but I definitely do remember that for a while—she was like "a catch."*

(Five or six minutes later, he added the following:)

. . . Going back to what I was saying about [he referred to the woman he came to think of as amazonlike], *you know, I hadn't thought of it before, but you've got to believe that's like other kinds of things—I mean, like, I've said—lots of men say—about some really successful ladies, you know, "She needs it," or maybe, "I bet she could be really something."*

Stanley's ambivalence toward working women reflects the influence of man-servant syndrome. Even as they become repulsively threatening, inaccessible "amazons," these women's accomplishments have a paradoxical allure. A number of factors might be causing this special, if short-lived, attraction: Ms. Employee's achievements, "despite her natural lack of ability as a woman," make her especially worthy of his offerings; he fantasizes that Ms. Employee has a special bounty that will anoint him when his man-servant deeds are done; she is able to take care of him (which his self-doubt makes appealing), and also influence others to believe that he is a special man since he "has" such a special woman. Over the long haul, however, Ms. Employee is only mortal, as all women are; none has any magically affirming bounty to take away a man's doubts. And no one should be surprised if, on some fateful morning, a man like Stanley packs his bags and moves on to relationships that seem less threatening.

Dr. Alice Thena understands man-servant syndrome and refuses to fall prey to its seductions. We were discussing Dr. Thena's role as a professional woman in a work setting that is still largely dominated by men. She described the men's ambivalence toward her, and, to follow up her thoughts, I asked her directly whether she had experiences that led her to believe that success in her field increased her allure.

Yes, but then of course it gets twisted by the underside of it—and that's a very interesting dynamic: There are men who need to protect me, as a more powerful woman, so that they can see **themselves** *as more powerful men. But underneath that dynamic they are needing to be taken care of by that more powerful woman.*

("To be taken care of?")

That's right. The need to protect always has an underside of dependency.

(I asked if that was related to something that she'd said earlier, namely that men are "looking to become men by what women can give them.")

That's right . . . because there is a characteristic interaction— you can tell when it's happening: A man is attracted to you because of who you are, what you do, what your accomplishments are. He finds a way to move into your professional life and then he starts needing more and more. And if you don't pay enough attention to him, he becomes petulant and self-pitying.

(I asked Dr. Thena for an example. She didn't hesitate a second.)

A junior male colleague who claims he can do a lot for me, and talks to me about all the things he is going to do for me. . . . He's never able to talk about just collaboration. Only . . . to talk about it in terms of what he can do for me. The more I engage with him, the happier he is, but if I detach and say, "I'll do this part myself," or "I have something else to do," he becomes enraged. Much more angry than the situation calls for.

("What do you think he's experiencing when you detach in this way?")

Well, he would say, "After all I've done for her." That's the sentence he would utter. . . . I'm saying to him, "Go off and play by yourself now. I don't need you at the moment." I think that's what's involved.

("When he says, 'After all I've done for you,' what is his hope, his fantasy?")

That I will be grateful and look up to him . . . I will make him a man.

Maintaining the illusion of women's dependency and lack of competence is essential to a man-servant's search for masculinity. He cannot serve a woman in the necessary way— by fulfilling the demands of the masculine competency cluster—if "she's her own man." By letting Ms. Employee know her place, she is transformed from a **person** who can do the "work of civilization," and thereby acquire the cluster's material bounty on her own, into a **woman** who concerns herself with "family and sexual life" and possesses the desired libidinal bounty.

Get Thee to a Kitchen

Men influenced by man-servant syndrome are compelled to experience work as unnatural for women. Their view of women is that, regardless of whatever else they may be doing, women's natural role in society is to use their socio-emotional bounty in the service of "their man" and the family. They believe that a woman's chief source of satisfaction arises from enriching others through bestowing her libidinal bounty: "Women *naturally* feel the responsibility to smooth life's bumps and make their families happy." Guided by this assumption, these men conclude that unmarried, "unattached" women cannot possibly be satisfied, nor can they fulfill their natural role because they lack both a "man" and a family. Is it any wonder that the words "spinster" and "old maid," unlike the word "bachelor," carry such strong negative connotations.

When they patronize working women, men are transforming them into mere carriers of libidinal bounty by implying, "This is too hard for you because you don't belong. You are handicapped and need help—a *real* man's help." When men designate some jobs as "O.K. for women," this is just another form of patronizing them, inasmuch as it tells women they need help because they are unsuited for doing the "work of civilization," i.e., man's work. Such patronization maintains work genderfication just as much as outright discrimination against hiring and promoting women. By both patronizing women and physically excluding them from work, men affected by the syndrome are able to maintain the illusion that they control the routes to prestige and power that they need in order to win women's affirming bounty.

Popular and scholarly media have supported men's efforts to patronize women and maintain work genderfication by portraying domestic work as easy and stress-free compared with "men's work." Being a wife, mother, or homemaker is typically characterized as a natural activity for women, something that they are created to do, that they want to do—and without any personal cost. When women go to work, they do so *in addition to* their "natural" work as women, or after they have completed their "natural" duties, or as a less than desirable substitute for what is "naturally" satisfying to them. In any event, work is unnatural, stressful, and something men should help women to avoid if possible.

This line of argument puts women into the kitchen. It says, even if women are out in the work world, the kitchen is where they belong: It suits their abilities and is better for their health. Actually, the only people it suits are those who want to maintain work genderfication. Research shows that women who stay at home suffer a level of stress that is certainly comparable to the stress people suffer at work. Indeed, when it comes to such symptoms as depression, evidence clearly indicates that women who stay home suffer more than those people who go to work.

The genderfication of work victimizes women while paradoxically increasing men's sense of vulnerability. Dr. Alice Thena told me the following story:

In a meeting with a peer . . . we're trying to decide policy for the center in which I work . . . it's clear that the male I'm working with does not know as much about the content as I do. He's new to the center. He's new to the discipline—untrained—but he's simply unable to hear anything that I say. Instead, he needs to placate me and says, "Gee, that's a really good idea—that's a really good idea." And it has nothing to do with the content of what I'm saying. . . . He pats me on the head. Placates me. Patronizes me. But cannot absorb anything that I'm saying in a meaningful way.

("By doing that, what do you think he thinks he's accomplishing?")

He believes that women need to be flattered—not heard—not understood—flattered. It's his job to do the flattering. If he does not flatter women he is not doing his job.

("He's not doing his job?")

Relating as a man.

("His flattering is instrumental to his becoming a man?")
That's correct.
("And how does he know when he has become a man?")
If I smile or respond coyly, he has done his job. He's made more masculine.
("What you give him, as a woman, makes him more masculine?")
That's right.
("So, in his mind, you have the capacity to make him masculine.")
Or to emasculate him!

When he is working with women, just as when he is romancing them, the man-servant puts himself into a self-constructed hell that strengthens the syndrome's grip on his life. It starts out as a neat little package: A woman cannot do men's work, therefore I'll help her to do it. That will keep her in her place and give me the opportunity to prove myself worthy of her bounty. But the package inevitably falls apart. Man-servants' helping is instrumental. It diminishes and controls women. But because the helping is instrumental, these men have given women the power to judge their masculinity. The men are waiting for women's bounty, a smile or coy response, and that makes them vulnerable. They have placed into women's hands the power of emasculation.

As self-doubt grows and the syndrome is fueled, other circumstances conspire to cause the package to continue to fall apart: Women haven't the power that these men fantasize they have: to affirm them, to wipe away all doubts. (Women no more have such power than men have the power to sweep women into their arms, put them on some great white charger, and carry them off in Prince-Charming fashion to their castles in the clouds to live happily ever after.) And women, like Ms. Employee, who are feeling most autonomous and independent, cannot long endure with amused tolerance man-servants' efforts to keep them in the kitchen.

In the end, man-servant, the victimizer of women, feels that *he* is a victim of women's ingratitude. His lament: "After all that I've done for her!"

I asked Dr. Alice Thena about women's responses to the kind of helping that man-servants do. Her answer shows how the syndrome twists the master-servant roles around until they are indistinguishable one from the other.

She began by describing what other women have told her about men's behavior at work. The "he" she is speaking of is a generic "he" and refers to men that women have told her about.

He doesn't really listen to me. He won't engage in the solution of the problem. He'll simply say, "Don't worry your pretty little head about it." And he won't let me manage my own career. He says, "Don't worry honey, stick with me, your career will be fine . . . I'll take care of you."

("And how do women like you respond?")

I think we . . . know that initially when we see this behavior, we can't say, "Could we cut this out and get on with it?" because that would be too offensive to the men. . . . We hope that as they get to know us that they will need to protect us less so that they can get to know us more, and it's more fun for us. But if it continues beyond what we think is a reasonable time, we just dismiss them.

(I pointed out to Dr. Thena that, for men seeking women's affirmation of their masculinity, dismissal is very likely the most painful and enraging thing a woman can do. To me, her sighing, seven-word response to this observation captures the weariness that women like her feel with men affected by the syndrome as well as indicates the sense of vulnerability and futility that fills the lives of those who have the syndrome.)

Yeah. They don't like it a lot.

BE A MAN, DON'T
ACT LIKE ONE

Man-servant syndrome is not a terminal condition. Steven Galli's life provides evidence of that. I introduced Steven in an earlier chapter, as an example of someone with Man-Servant Syndrome, Style: Educator.

You may remember that Steven's first wife was much younger than he. According to Steven, before they met, her life had been sheltered. Her father was strict. Her mother was passive. The family lived in a small town located in America's heartland. During my interview with him, Steven acknowledged that his relationship with his wife, as her "teacher" and "guide," perpetuated the domination and dependency of those sheltered childhood years.

Initially, Steven's experience of the educator role was positive, even sexually arousing. Later, when he had to reap what he had sown, Steven grew ambivalent about his man-servant educator role. Its attraction was being offset by a building resentment that he was bearing the family's entire burden of responsibility for making decisions. And he was, because that is exactly the way he had set it up.

"Ambivalence" is the key word to understanding what Steven was experiencing. It foretells what happened when his wife eventually rebelled against the way he exercised control over her life: Rather than feeling relieved at the opportunity to lift his "burden of complete responsibility," Steven felt as resentful of her rebellion as he did of her dependency. He and his wife divorced after more than two decades of marriage. Sometime later Steven remarried, and he was happy to tell me about his second wife.

. . . The woman I am now married to has a master's degree. . . . She is very bright, very energetic, very outgoing. I would almost say the flip side [compared to his first wife]. I've thought about this often. We often say, "We repeat our mistakes." I didn't in this case. I went all the way over on the other side. Strong woman, much younger. She's twenty years younger than I am. . . . She's perfectly willing to help, to nurture. If I'm not talking about something, she sits me down and says, "O.K. Let's talk." So, she will drive the nurturing part of the thing. Insist on it. Pull me out. . . . Very much of a peer. Much more outgoing. I'm willing to say to her, "I'm really pissed off. I don't feel good about what's happening." A lot of this has to do with what happened to me in the interim too. I'm willing to share myself more with her. . . . Be more of a whole person.

(I asked Steven to tell me more about why it was that with his first wife he was less willing to say, "I'm pissed off." His response is evidence of how the syndrome imprisons men as well as women.)

Yeah, I felt like she couldn't handle it. The relationship was one of—well, the way I saw it at the time—dependency. I had to *be the strong, stalwart keeper of the family, so to speak, and I couldn't allow my vulnerability to show through. Or, at least, I felt like I couldn't.* And I felt like, *if I did, somehow or other it would spoil the image of the family that we* [note the self-correction here] *that I had created—at least in my mind.*

. . . bullshit, of course, but that's the way I had it at the time. Whereas I got some real viewpoints of myself in the ensuing years, and I found out that I'm not really all as unique as I thought I was—all as strong as I thought I was—or as self-sustaining— that I needed someone as much as they needed me—God!—willing to ask for help—to share myself.

("Is there jeopardy in doing that?")

No. As a matter of fact, I found out that because of who she was, and is, that she needed to know what was going on inside of me . . . as much as I needed to know what was going on inside of her. And, as opposed to destroying the relationship, or damaging it, or diminishing it, it strengthened it.

Man-servant syndrome is not a terminal condition. Steven Galli's experiences are an illustration of that. There is a remedy. But undoing man-servant syndrome is not a matter of taking two aspirin and lots of liquid, and getting some bed rest. Neither I nor anyone else can provide you with the ten, handy-dandy, easy-to-use, foolproof steps to a happy life free of man-servant syndrome. I wish that I could, but I cannot. What I can do, however, is tell you about the struggles of men and women who have learned to manage the syndrome and to extract from their stories, ideas that will be useful to us all.

My conversations with 150 men and women have led me to recognize the need for men's emotional emancipation. Breaking the bonds of man-servant syndrome requires an internal struggle against the excessive expectations spawned by the masculine competency cluster; it requires confronting the self-doubt men inevitably experience when they fail to fulfill those expectations; it requires disengaging from the fantasy that women possess a healing, emotional bounty that they will yield to men who serve them according to the cluster's specifications; and it requires challenging the disillusionment and rage men direct toward women who "fail" to give their "bounty" to them, "after all that men have done for them."

Relationships in which the struggle for emotional emancipation has been won possess five guiding declarations. Each of these declarations can be expressed in only a few words, but do not let their brevity fool you. Any one of the Ten Commandments also contains only a few words, but those words are heavy with implication, and they are notoriously difficult to carry out. The five guiding declarations of men's emotional emancipation are nothing like the moral equivalent of the Ten Commandments, but they too prove easier to applaud than to practice:

- Be a man, don't act like one.
- Prevent one person's burden from becoming another's beacon.
- Giving means more than doing.
- Work the boundaries.
- Facilitate talk among men, not man-talk.

I want to tell you about some men and women who have struggled to express these declarations in their lives together. From their experiences we can learn at least two useful lessons: First, we can learn how to recognize man-servant syndrome's danger signals when they appear in our own lives; and second, when the signals do appear, we can learn how to respond in ways that offer us a better chance of building more mutually satisfying male-female relationships that are less frequently punctuated by man-servant syndrome's destructive cycles.

Be a Man, Don't Act Like One

It is late afternoon. One of my three daughters, Alison, who is nearly ten years old, has arrived home from school. As I walk through our apartment toward my desk, I notice that she is watching television. I pause in the doorway, we chat, and then we are both distracted by the program being broadcast.

We are watching a sitcom. The TV screen fills with a man's face, then with a woman's. The man and woman appear to be living in the same modest house. Are they man and wife? Are they regular characters? I don't know. (At the time I didn't know the show's name, and I still don't.)

My ignorance is not complete, however. After hearing only a few lines of the script, I recognize the plot and the pernicious cliché about men it contains: Men are tyrants who bumble domestic chores, show no emotion except anger, and are helplessly compelled to come to the aid of needy women. (The plot also maligns women. One of the characters is a buxom blond neighbor. Her voice is soft and throaty. And her manner is concerned and sympathetic. She seems able to soothe the lead male character, who has been tense because of work troubles. In an apparent swoon, she declares her conviction in his competence, and speaks to

him about a problem that she "simply cannot handle."
Hint: Will he help? Does he resist, or even hesitate? On the
contrary, he swells with strength, eager to become her
champion and fulfill this soft, inviting woman's needs.)

The sitcom's plot and its characters reflect and support a
social blueprint for gender behavior. It is society's script for
men and women. According to the script, men's role is to
fulfill the prescription expressed in the masculine competency cluster by providing male-female relationships with
what some scholars have called *agency*. "Real men," the
prescription declares, are supposed to possess independence
and self-reliance. They should be aggressive, ambitious, and
competitive. "Real men" are leaders. They are dominant,
forceful, and instrumental. "Real men" take initiative, spe-
cialize in analytical thinking, and they do not show feminine traits such as weakness or emotion.

A woman's role is different. Instead of agency, women
provide what has been called *communion:* Women are nurturant and compassionate. They should be affectionate, gentle, and empathic. In relationships with others they are
cooperative and interpersonally sensitive.

Men with man-servant syndrome play their role according to society's script. They are forced to engage in this
pretense because they are trying to fulfill a prescription for
"manhood" that is impossible to fulfill. Ironically, as each
effort to act like a man falls short of the forever elusive,
excessive, idealized standards of the masculine competency
cluster, so does self-doubt grow, producing still more pressure to keep up the pretense and act like a man.

Men with man-servant syndrome are trapped in a deadly
spiral because they believe that what can free them from
painful, growing doubts about their masculinity is women's

affirming bounty, which women reserve for "real men only." What these men do not understand is that only in fairy tales do frogs become princes because they earn a maiden's affection. In reality, if you feel like a frog inside, no one but you can make you feel less repulsive.

Man-servants play the prescribed role almost all of the time. Few men can claim a lifelong experience of turning down the part. At some point, every man has tried to play the "proper" role.

Consider the case of Fred Comb. He was a youthful victim of man-servant syndrome.

I was in college . . . it was a very intense relationship the end of which was very devastating to me. It was very much a life-changing sort of thing, a growing-up thing. The relationship was one where the woman involved . . . played a role of being very girlish, and coy, and sort of cuddling, and childish, and needing to be taken care of. I mean, that is the role that I think she took on in the relationship. And it was one that made me feel big, and important, and protective, now that I speak about it. I frankly didn't start talking about that relationship thinking that thought, but now that we're talking about it, it did feel that way.

(I asked him whether her behavior was appealing.)

It was enormously appealing to me . . . in terms of an emotional involvement that was blinding [me] to almost everything that was going on around me. Probably the most intense emotional relationship, romantically, that I've had with a woman.

. . . We met at a college mixer. I noticed her eyes. . . . She was attractive. She was petite. She was self-possessed. There was a lot of self-confidence that radiated from this person. This may sound a little inconsistent with the girlish, coy sort of thing, but it somehow wasn't. I mean, she wasn't brassy, but in terms of brash

132   HARVEY A. HORNSTEIN, PH.D.

display of self-confidence—you just sort of knew this person had a sense of presence and self, and you could pick that up in the animation in her face.

(I tried to understand more about this curious contradiction in his experience of her attributes. So I said questioningly, "And yet there was a little-girl–like quality?")

*Very much—which she played out. I can't remember particular behavioral things, but there would be . . . soft of little, cute, playful things in the way she would behave toward me, and letters would have little drawings on them and things like that. There were a lot of little coquettish behaviors. . . . There were little "gifty" sorts of things that would arrive. I'm sure there are ways in which I was sort of **shown off** when I would show up where she was at school that had something of that quality in it and—I'm groping for the recollections but I don't find any more detail right now.*

("What did it do for you?")

What did it do for me? That's a real tough question 'cause I'm really not quite sure. I know it made me feel very good . . . not in just a warm and fuzzy way but . . . in terms of my focus and energy level and just sort of firing out on all cylinders. Everything was going just absolutely right in terms of my life. . . . I mean, I was very focused and energized. So obviously, it was doing something for me that carried over into my life beyond the relationship. It probably just made me feel good about life. It made me want to do good things!

(I wondered about how this "perfect" relationship was pushing him toward being a "perfect" man. I asked, "To do good things?")

Yes. Just to be the best I could be. I don't know whether I was trying to prove something to her or whether I was doing it because I was motivated by her, but I was very clearly motivated at the time. . . . I mean, I've always had motivation to be very achiev-

ing. But I don't know, I'm groping for what else it might have done for me and why I might have felt that way about my life. I guess the other thing was I sort of felt that I had it made. Everything just felt right and good, and it just—WOW—if life could just be like this all the time . . . "Had it made" is the right phrase. It was just all whole.

(I said, "Being together with her made you feel whole, complete, in a positive way. In a way that left you feeling elated?")

Yeah. "Elated" is exactly the right word. And elated not just in her presence, but every day when I got up. It was a very positive period of time.

(There was a magic to the relationship. She was "there" even when she wasn't, and Fred performed for her through most of his waking hours. I commented, "She was present, even if she wasn't there physically.")

Yeah, that was part of my life.

("It was part of your life," I concurred, and then asked again, "How did you respond to this little-girl quality? What did you become when she became a little girl?")

I guess . . . I was the big protector. I do remember her saying this would have mattered to her—that she saw me at this mixer— that she had this feeling—using an expression that was current then, and still may be, that I was BMOC [Big Man On Campus]. I mean, she just thought that I was important and so on, and she tried to, I think, nurture that feeling. . . . I'm sure her wanting me to have those sorts of aspects probably made me feel good.

(I inquired whether he had become the protector. His response shows just how much "acting like a man" was an important part of his relationship with this woman.)

I'm struggling with that. "Protector" isn't quite the right word.

You know, I can picture sort of hugging her and sort of—
"protecting" comes to mind, but it isn't quite the right word because
I wasn't protecting her from anything. **But I was the bigger**
and superior force—I guess—that is more the idea than
the protector—a potential protector.

Nearly two decades have passed since Fred Comb imagined
that he was a "potential protector." Data from public opinion polls and other forms of research tell us that society
seems to be scripting a new role for men. It is a role that
includes attributes that were formerly reserved for women.
Some men now feel freer to be nurturant, sensitive, cooperative, and gentle. For them, family and personal relationships are growing in importance in comparison to work and
achievements. This new role is less macho, and more an-
drogynous. It does not require men to act like the competency cluster's idealized "real men," but encourages them to
be people whose behavior fluctuates from agency to communion, and back again, as different situations require.

Oddly, in addition to all its potential benefits for gender
relationships, the new script has also given rise to a particularly well-camouflaged expression of man-servant syndrome. In fact, I interviewed several men who seem to be
playing the new role but, in reality, are still acting according to the old prescriptions.

The single most important clue in recognizing men possessed by this new form of man-servanting is the humorless,
driven commitment that men now have to behave in ways
that were previously considered "for women only." Danny
Alterwine, twenty-four years old and divorced, is preparing
for a career in the restaurant industry.

*   *   *

*Missy was an incredibly beautiful woman. I loved to just look at her—gaze. From the first, it was, you know, I **decided** that it wasn't going to be any ordinary relationship.*

(I let the "I decided" pass. In retrospect, given what else he had to say, that expression might certainly be interpreted as a sign of man-servant syndrome.)

. . . I watched my father—for years—with my mother. It was a real macho scene. Like, he gave her nothing. Feeling, emotion. He was a provider. But as a person, a companion, you know [his head-shaking, nonverbal no finished the sentence]. *She really needed us—my sister—and I was the oldest, so it was really important. And it's probably when I learned, decided, that it was going to be different.*

(In order to bring him back to the relationship that he was discussing, I asked, "With Missy, you decided that it would be different?")

Yeah. None of that old nonsense. The traps. But she never caught on. She wasn't ready for it.

("Not ready for it?")

No—no way!

("What was 'it'?")

*Well, like, I wasn't about to do the male things just because I was a man. . . . If she could have gotten into that, it would've been great. I was doing my bit, but she couldn't see it. She wasn't ready for that kind of partner and I got no **gratitude** for what I was doing—the effort.*

Danny Alterwine's giving to Missy was instrumental. He wanted something from her in return: "If she could have gotten into that, it would've been great," he said. Make no mistake about it, dogmatically "liberated" men like Danny are performing. Although their behavior is different, their motivation is the same as that of their more traditional counterparts. Their behavior possesses the controlling rigidity of men who are afflicted by the syndrome and are driven by the fantasy of what they need to do for women to secure their bounty in return. Men who are successful in dealing with man-servant syndrome show greater fluidity and flexibility in their relationships with women.

I asked Dr. Alice Thena to tell me about the character of relationships she has had with men who were reasonably free of the syndrome. (Of course, I asked the question by describing the syndrome's symptoms, not by using the term.) Her characterization of these more positive male-female relationships contrasts sharply with Danny Alterwine's description of the relationship he had with his wife. At first, what she says may surprise you because it seemingly supports a conformity to traditional stereotypes of gender-appropriate behavior. But as you read on, you will learn that Dr. Thena recognizes that freedom from the syndrome is marked by a capacity to behave comfortably in different ways, some of which are stereotypical, some not.

[The stereotypical behaviors] *are common ground because* [women] *are brought up that way too. It's one of the shared beliefs. It's social lubrication. We both know how to behave initially. . . . It's a commonality rather than a difference.*

(I asked her to explain why in some relationships, stereotypical male behavior is destructive, but in other relationships, that is not so.)

If that's all there is. . . . The best example I can give of that is a contract. . . . No one wants to be in a role all the time. When people trade off, it's usually comfortable and that's not an issue. Some people take charge in some situations and others take charge in

other situations, and it works out. But . . . when some people . . .
are always protectees rather than protectors, you get a lot of conflict.
In heterosexual relationships, when you don't want to negotiate,
you can always fall back on the social role, and that makes it
easier, without thinking about it. . . . When Donald [her hus-
band] *and I are both exhausted, and have to drive home, he will*
drive.

("You don't even talk about who sits on which side of the
car?")

Don't even talk about it.

("So he takes care.")

He takes care in that way, and ultimately, when the house is a
mess, and we are both exhausted, I will take care.

("You straighten up.")

That's right. Without even thinking about it. It's my job, not
his. . . . Yet, it is a very egalitarian household. We tried to fill
out a form [which] *asked who was the primary caretaker—parents*
of [her child]. *I mean, you can count the hours, but it's only*
because he [her husband] *has a longer commute.*

("Otherwise you cannot make the distinction?")

Absolutely not. There are these teeny-weeny things that we just
take for granted, that really have nothing to do with his role as
protector or my role as helper.

Men and women who deal successfully with the syndrome
respond to the moment, sometimes with agency and sometimes with communion. Their behavior is neither fixed by
prescription nor fueled by a fantasy of what their mates
should give in return for the "gifts" they have received.

Compare the thoughts and feelings of Danny Alterwine
and Fred Comb with those of Bobby Soprisa, a forty-six-
year-old police officer.

* * *

. . . I always end up getting very close to the people I work with. And the people I'm less effective in dealing with are the kinds of people who don't let me get close to them. And I've been very fortunate throughout an eighteen-year career now, working with many superiors and literally hundreds of subordinates, to pretty much be able to do that. . . . It's those close personal relationships that I find are most satisfying, and probably more so than the work itself.

I've had those relationships, obviously mostly with men that I've worked with—because that's been the predominance of the people I'm dealing with—but the women that I've dealt with, by and large, certainly have seemed more willing to risk that vulnerability to get to know someone beyond the superficial level.

(He continued by telling me what was rewarding in these relationships.)

*. . . As I think about it, what is most fulfilling is realizing that they want to know more of the **real me** and not just the figurehead or whatever they see in the position that I am in. And that knowing process most often occurs through lots of casual encounters through the course of the official, professional day. Sharing anecdotes about your life or kidding around, but all the while getting a little bit below the surface and to know . . . that someone is reacting to me. . . .*

The **me** is Bobby Soprisa, not his uniform, rank, or gender-linked prescription of either who he should be, or who a woman should be in relation to him. The Bobby Soprisas of this world are free to be men because they do not feel compelled to act like men. They are more or less initiating, analytic, nurturant, or compassionate, depending on circumstance and ability, not on a prescription of what one must be to be a "real man."

Prevent One Person's Burden from Becoming Another's Beacon

Colette Dowling, author of *The Cinderella Complex,* writes of women, "Most of us have not yet made a true decision about our lives. Trying to maintain a situation in which we give up neither our independence nor our dependence drains us of energy. Consciously, we blame men for not changing, but unconsciously we're quite willing to have them stay the way they are [p. 210]."

There is a counterpart to Dowling's observation about women that applies to men. Often without any recognition of the propelling forces, many men are either ambivalent about the changing role of women, or they flat-out don't want it to occur because it would destroy what they imagine is a means of affirming their masculinity. After all, what would men do if they believed that women were capable of being autonomous and competent? For whom would they provide and protect? How would they earn the credits necessary to obtain women's bounty and erase their own doubts?

Men who are either ambivalent about the changing role of women or simply opposed to it are attracted to stereotypical female behavior: They respond to hints of neediness and dependency just as moths do to the light of a distant, flickering flame. Thus, women's culturally driven dependency, which men have historically fostered and exploited, is not simply a burden for women. It is also a beacon for men who feel the pull of man-servant syndrome.

A faint "You're so strong," or "I need someone like you to take care of me," is commonly all that is required to push these men over the edge. In this way, the ambivalent Cinderellas that Dowling writes about attract male behavior, which in turn creates more pressure on women to continue to accept their Cinderella-like dependency and domination by men.

Linda Belsur, a twenty-eight-year-old secretary, recounted for me her initial experiences with William.

*He had to be a **man**. Can you understand that? I sensed that's where it was for him. At the time I thought so—later to be proven wrong—very wrong—I may have created a Frankenstein, but I learned my lesson. . . . Probably it started with him stopping for my car. Like I told you, it had broken down and I was doing this number: "Oh, you're such a good mechanic." Which was exactly true. He was a plumber—or worked for one. . . .*

("If he's a good mechanic, what's wrong with telling him that?")

*What's wrong? Why, it's not the mechanic that I was talking to, if you see what I mean. It was the **ma-an**. I was flipping my eyes, swishing my hips—it wasn't what I was saying. IT— WAS—WHAT—I—WAS—SAYING: "You big man, me little girl!" And from there on, that man had to live up to it. He tried—impossible—no.*

Linda Belsur saw her stereotypical behavior as a beacon for William. It attracted him, and he behaved in response to the signals she was sending. Without a word, a deal was struck. He would act as a "man" should act, and in return she would be a dependent, grateful woman. In her own view, Linda created a "Frankenstein" monster. (Frankenstein's monster is an interesting symbol: Not clearly a man—being neither dead nor alive—he is composed of parts garnered from men's corpses.) In the end, in order to rid herself of the creature, William, she had to destroy the relationship.

Tom Granman, a government employee, talked about his encounters with women at work. His experiences parallel Linda's, but they reflect the other side of the coin and illustrate how some men will not let the burden sexism has produced in women become their beacon.

I've worked professionally with [two women] *and both have been close friends. . . . For any professional or personal problem, they use me in a very dependent way to help them solve all these messes that they get into. . . . I felt like that was my responsibility, particularly if it was with women who were in need and whatever—but, as I say, increasingly I've gotten to the place where I don't like it.*

("You don't like it?")

I mean—that doesn't mean that I don't like trying to solve what I consider a real problem for somebody, or being supportive, or whatever. I have another friend, Sharon, who I think is an adult, mature person. [She] *has lots of problems—and she falls apart occasionally—and then really turns to me for advice. . . . For just whatever reason, I don't resent that because it feels like when I give her advice, or help solve a problem, there's a real process there, where the other person is interested, and it's going to go somewhere.*

With these other [two women] *it seems like it's more—I think it's a game or a process where the point is to keep this dependent sort of relationship going, rather than the notion that there's a solution to a problem. . . . You really get the sense with them that they're almost junkies. I mean, that they thrive on your intervening in the drama of their lives, and taking care of them, and fixing it up for them, and so on. And it's almost frustrating when it gets fixed up because then they have to be responsible people.*

*   *   *

Maurice Mandar's wife also sent signals about what kind of a man she wanted him to be. He saw the signals and, initially, he was more than willing to be guided by them. But in time, when other experiences gave him fresh understanding of the implications of his behavior for himself, his wife, and their relationship, he tried to steer away from this beacon. Unfortunately, it was too late, the relationship could not avoid the shoals of marital disaster. Here is Maurice's description of the event:

. . . *As it turned out, she had hoped to convert me, which I never suspected.*

("Into what?" I asked.)

Well, into what her idea of what a man should be like, which was much more working class, not so intellectual. So that we had—I think we had key words that we would throw at each other. I can't remember what they were. Her notion was that anybody who was like me, was not a "regular guy."

("She didn't think you were a regular guy?")

Right. I think what she meant was, in fact, that I thought of myself as better than truck drivers, pub brawlers, whatever. And a regular guy is someone who's just a Democrat or whatever. **God knows, I tried to fit in.** *Actually, I thought that I was doing pretty well. . . . I mean, with one group of people [at school] and another group of people [at home]. And so—I also thought of her as being uncouth in her refusal to go past a certain point.* (Here, he was speaking both as a man-servant and as someone with insight into the way men's and women's burdens become their mates' or partners' beacons.)

I think that there was a certain excitement in difference. It was an exoticness that fueled passion and sexuality, and all that sort of thing, and need. And there was an awful lot that each of us experienced, and we had ways of looking at things that the other was ignorant of. It was sort of like meeting people from different countries. Well, what happened was that when the novelty started to wear off, the amount of common ground that there was, was enormously small. So that there was less and less to talk about. . . . I would be spending hours in an activity that she simply could not understand why anyone could find so fascinating. . . . So, all I was doing [from her point of view] was sitting in the house being an absentee. And, conversely, there was only so much hanging out with friends with beer and card-playing that I could do. I can't believe, as a matter of fact, that the two of us got involved in the first place. . . .

Yeah, it gradually just came apart in a way that just had no crisis to it. It probably was held together for a year or two by guilt. Neither of us was quite ready to say, "I have had it, and I don't want this anymore, and I'm going." Each of us imagined that that's what would have to be said. And, in fact, it was fascinating. When I was the one who said, "That's it," her reaction was, "All this time and now you're going."

(Maurice was no longer willing to play the part prescribed by the masculine competency cluster. He was no longer willing to respond to the beacon that his wife was flashing. And he was no longer willing to be a beacon flashing guidance to his wife. I encouraged him again to speak about what she wanted him to be that he no longer desired to be.)

I wasn't the salt of the earth. . . . It was a double assault— one was the magic kingdom, which was supposed to leave her open-mouthed, wasn't having that effect. [Despite his initial promises, her Prince Charming had not transformed her into a princess dwelling happily forever after.] *The other one was that because I could do anything* [he laughed aloud here, showing that he recognized that these words were an irrational residue of man-servant syndrome], *I was sure that I was the salt of the earth. . . . My view of it was that I could enter the world as a truck driver and be at home there as easily as I could enter the world of the museumgoer.*

(Earlier in the interview he had referred to Hollywood images of Gary Cooper, Alan Ladd, and Humphrey Bogart as male heroes, capable of doing it all, so now I asked, "Like Coop and Ladd and Bogart?")

Right. Coop would shoot it out with the bad guys. He was Sergeant York, and he was the architect from The Fountainhead. *So, oh God, I wouldn't be twenty years old for anything again; not for anything in the world.*

(I assured him, "You don't have to be." His response was only two words, proclaiming both his personal insight and obvious relief at being relatively free of man-servant syndrome's temptations and burdens.)

I know!

Giving Means More Than Doing

At one point in my conversation with Dr. Alice Thena, she spoke about how some men handle the emotional give-and-take of male-female relationships:

They are so busy protecting that they don't give much of themselves. They protect instead of being genuine. And I would say that it is also the way they are friends of women—you never get to know who they really are. You never hear much about them. You don't hear much about their fears, their concerns, or their anxieties. If you talk to them about what's going on in their lives, they sound like they're managing. They always sound like they're managing.

Men troubled by man-servant syndrome would probably find Alice Thena's comments bewildering. In response, they might be inclined to ask, "How do you really get to **know** these men? Hear about **them**? Learn about their fears, concerns, or anxieties?" and then they might answer by saying, "You don't. It's ridiculous to wonder about these things. Men are supposed to manage. They are supposed to be in control and decisive. **It's what women want and need.** Expressing fear, concern, or anxiety would undermine men's role. They would lose women's respect."

In their relationships with women men affected by the syndrome understand *giving* to mean *doing*. *Doing* is what acting as a man means. *Doing* earns what a woman has to give. *Doing* is part of an exchange. Its purpose is instrumental—to get something from women in return—and does not involve selflessly sharing part of oneself.

What men give to women depends on their style of man-servanting: *Ministers* give to women by *doing for* them. They provide. Providing, to ministers, is the key to receiving the women/goddesses' bounty. *Educators'* giving emphasizes *doing to* women. Educators develop, teach, and guide women (those unfortunate diamonds in the rough) in order to get their fantasized libidinal bounty. *Lancelots* give by performing. They *do in front of* women, hoping that women will find the deeds acceptable and acknowledge them by giving their affirming bounty in return.

Man-servants give in order to get. When shouting

matches erupt, they feel justified in claiming, "After all I've done for you!" recounting with the zeal of an accountant the **things** that were given, and feeling bewildered by women's counter-claims about "feeling alone," "without a partner," or like "someone who is taken for granted."

Manny Delsol, a musician, was shocked to hear a woman tell him such things. The occasion marked the beginning of his transition away from man-servant syndrome.

. . . She is a very fine woman; the best, man, and it was like, Wow, you're talking about me. It was open ceiling and blue sky—light and sunshine—I could see. Man, was she ever right. Time for a change.

("What did she say, Manny? What caused the open ceiling, light, and sunshine?")

That I wasn't there. I mean, like, in feeling, touching—inside—you know. It was all outside. . . . I thought it was right. I was deep into my music. Working to develop something fine—a good sound. Working with some good people. It took time and . . . it went on for a couple of years. And, you know, like—well, she said, "You bring home surprises"—whatever—little gifts—a flower—something special—"but those are things, Manny, outside things. Like, inside, you're not there. You're into a whole scene, but I'm not part of it."

("How did you respond to that?")

It was our scene. Not just for me. What was happening, was happening for two—more for her—my life. Like, her people, they were not pleased with me as a choice. There was a need to make her proud. I wanted to be special for this fine woman. Music is what I've got . . . I mean, now I know it's not so. But well, then, man, I was going to bring home the bacon, just like any blue-suit,

Wall-Street, red-blooded, American-capitalist, male, top-floor-office executive.

("Bacon? You mean, things such as money?")

Money. Sure, it could be money. But bacon is bacon, man. It's just stuff to eat. It's a thing that men give to women—on the table, in bed, jewelry—it's bacon—important friends. "Don't you worry your pretty little head." It's all bacon, right.

I was sick and didn't know it. Filled with . . . a social disease. I got it from something—screwed over—and didn't know. I thought I was healthy. . . . So, I said to myself, "I am not going to lose this fine woman." I cried, Harvey. I cried, and opened up, like never before. We went on to five, six, in the morning. Just sharing all the things that scared me, that she meant, everything. Like starting over again. She loved me, you see, and I wasn't there. Hey, how could I be—no one could love me. I had such negatives about [he pounded his chest with his fist, indicating that he had "negative" feelings about himself]. *I had to give her things because I couldn't give myself. How could I give something like that? I was not really making it.*

("No bacon?")

No bacon.

As is the case with so many men, Manny felt unworthy. He failed to measure up to the masculine competency cluster's idealized standards. Because he did not deserve to be affirmed by a woman for *who* he was, Manny behaved the way men with the syndrome typically do: He sought a woman's affection in exchange for *what* he could give her.

Manny was fortunate. The woman he was with chose not to be a beacon. She spoke out, convincing him that *giving* means more than *doing*. Bacon, in any form, was not what she most wanted. The thing that he had to bring home was himself. It is "open ceiling and blue sky," a lesson for us all.

Work the Boundaries

Men touched by man-servant syndrome do not want women in the work world. Even when women are physically present in work settings, they are psychologically dismissed by these men through the mechanism of **work genderfication.** When work is genderfied, it is experienced as being "for men only," and women are treated as visiting aliens. By crossing some invisible boundary, women have entered a world for which they lack the appropriate qualities. Whatever women may be doing in the "alien" man's world of work, they are doing it only as an add-on to everything else they *"ought to be doing."*

Work genderfication protects men by keeping women as "only women," no matter what level of success they reach. Because they are women, they are, at best, out of place and, at worst, freaks who look like women but lack the defining essence of femininity. Tucked away deep inside men who practice work genderfication is a suspicion, which creeps out in jokes and side comments: It is that these freakish women really await men, even crave men, who will provide for, guide, and dazzle them. "They really want it!"

Work genderfication puts women in their stereotypical place. What men deem women fit to take care of possesses less prestige than what men believe *they* are fit to take care of. *A woman cannot do man's work,* these men reason, *I'll help her to do it. It's what she really wants.* And the often unspoken by-product of this reasoning is *It will keep her in her place* [as man's subordinate], *and give me opportunity to prove myself worthy of her bounty.*

Paradoxically, work genderfication, which is intended to increase men's security, actually increases their vulnerability because women's responses, not men's inner conviction, become the determiners of their self-worth.

Leon Buscar, a personnel officer for a construction company, told me about an episode that helped him cross over the boundary that work genderfication places between men and women. This episode occurred when he was attending residential business meetings for his company, to which spouses were invited. His business associates were all male. None of their wives worked. Leon's wife, however, was a successful career woman. But in that situation, he explained, she was regarded as "his gal." At first, he was perfectly willing to let her be "his gal," because he was concerned about being seen as a "man" by his "tough, competent" associates. One way to be a "man," he said, was to let his wife be "my gal," simpering, empty-headed, and dependent.

. . . It was role-expected, or it was role-modeling on my part of what they were doing. It was interesting that what was happening . . . was [killing] *some of the positive things that I really valued. Here, I thought, she's a fantastic woman, and stunning, and attractive—smart as hell. You know, I just really liked to kind of show her off. But in showing her off I wasn't showing her off as being that fully multidimensional person. You know, it was a nice little marionette that walked, and talked, and looked good.*

("And if you could have that marionette that walked and talked and looked good, how would it affect you?")

It was ego gratification. People would say, "Damn, he did O.K." In the stereotypical sense. The fact that she had all the social graces and whatnot added to it. Besides being attractive, she had a mind, even if I didn't want to test it too much. What happened there . . . sometimes it was startling when she, in her own way, started saying "bullshit" in some of those situations. . . . Coming over to the men, saying, "Why are you doing it like that?" or talking about the education system. [His wife was an educator.]

You know, it's ubiquitous to think that everybody can run a school. "Well, [she'd say], *what would you do in this situation?" And rattle off three or four things that were probably more complicated than their current operating hassles. Some people were kind of shocked and, after a while, it'd go to the point where I was comfortable, and almost bemused by how she would play an audience, and almost . . . be a light attracting moths simply because they weren't used to encountering females that had strong opinions and ideas.*

And she could converse on a number of issues, and even had something to say about how they ought to do assembly-plant maintenance. . . . What kind of clinched it was when that started happening, I said, "Why did I worry? I must have been crazy." Now, my assignment of being an excellent [personnel person] *is enhanced because she is one in a very small number of women who are totally self-sufficient, who choose to get into mutually interdependent and loving relationships. . . . The couple of years it took for that transition to go were difficult, but once it happened, mmmmm.*

(I wanted to know more about the transition. I said, "At one point you felt that if you could have a sort of simpering, simple woman hanging on your arm, just looking stunning, you would somehow be enhanced. People would look at you and say, 'Hey, he's really O.K. because look at what he has.' But you learned that enhancement was really there when she was being intelligent, thoughtful, and questioning." He agreed and told me what happened when he relinquished the need to have her as "my gal," and she could feel free to be herself.)

There were instances where more value was assigned to us as a couple, and there was more of an attractiveness to have us around rather than the perfunctory "Well, let's invite position and spouse." "Hey," people would say, "Gloria's not with you?" Because then the expectation was she'd be there and it was a loss if she wasn't.

(The boundary was crossed. Leon learned that his masculinity was not boosted because his wife was reduced to being just "my gal." On the contrary, when he could accept work as simply work, not as man's world, he and his wife were able to support each other and learn from one another in ways that were impossible when separated by the boundary of work genderfication.)

*. . . What has happened is that we've become coaches and counselors with each other. And over seventeen years, we've grown more alike—knowing that she is more assertive now and absolutely a master, better than I am, in going into a situation, and just charming, and winning, and influencing people in a direct way. . . . What we've found is that I've really gained from her more of an intuitive sense for what's going on—in reading the subtleties—rather than just rashly proceeding on, and being able to put ideas down succinctly and clearly rather than just relying on the power to bullshit through anything. And a kind of blending there, I think, has made **both of us** stronger and successful.*

* * *

Marty Adams, a successful creator-producer of television programs, also felt more successful after he reached out to his wife across the boundary of work genderfication.

When I told Marty what the interview was going to be about, he immediately recognized the territory into which we would be venturing.

It's not easy because it's a very general question and it's also kind of personal. And also makes me evaluate a lot of stuff, some of which is not going to be that easy to talk about.

(Marty chose to tell me about his first independent project. It was very special to him.)

I didn't want this to be everybody's first [project]. *I wanted some support* [in Marty's field of work, the project editor is critical to the outcome being special], *so you become very, very close to your editor—if you're lucky—and together you really create a dialogue, a creative dialogue. But into that creative dialogue are brought a lot of important traits by both sides. A sense of humor, what's funny; what's vulgar; what's pretty; who's pretty; what the values of the* [project] *are; what the argument of the story is; what the audience for it is; . . . how are we sacrificing any one of these things by doing this, by doing that; if it's too long, do we pull it out? And you can imagine what happens. But—for someone like myself who has a tendency to internalize and somatize—almost to catastrophe—the identification with the material and the project is very, very, very strong. . . . Even if I pretend that it doesn't feel like that.*

(I started to say, "So, working with your wife as editor on this had important implications for the . . ." He finished the sentence.)

For the marriage, for the relationship, and for the career—the mutual career. And it has been fabulous and terrible.

("Tell me about both sides.")

Well, as you can imagine, I started this run-on sentence by saying, on a first [project] you are really exposed because you've never done it before. You are out there.

I cannot make an analogy for you except, imagine that you had never driven a car. And you had read all about it. You've heard about it. And you've seen people drive cars, but now somebody hands you the keys and says, "You've got to drive from your house here up to Yankee Stadium."

You know how you're going to be. After ten years, you do a lot of things automatically. You know when you should be frightened. You get a whole feel for yourself in traffic. Well, maybe that's not such a terrible analogy: The sense of danger, and the sense of risk, and all that is very, very real. Because you always think you're never going to get a second chance to [do a second project] if this one doesn't work—and it's your fault.

Well, anyway, you're confronted with all this and your savior, and your collaborator, in the solution of these problems is your editor.

(At first, Marty had recruited one of the business's best-known editors. But the dialogue and the stimulation that he had hoped for weren't there.)

So [the editor] and I parted and I asked Maura [Marty's wife] if she would come in and edit. She had never edited this kind of [project] before. . . . But she had the background to be more than just a listener. [It wasn't], "It's O.K., darling. Don't worry. I love you and you're the best." She had legitimate and valuable observations and contributions that came out of her own experience. . . . And it wasn't so much practical—like, "Why didn't you put the [equipment] over there?" or anything like that—but the sense that there was another person in my life who shared enough of the same values that I didn't think that I was completely crazy. . . . You know, emotional support, but more than that. . . . This was an educated, an informed opinion that I was fortunate enough to have around.

Maura had gone through this whole process with me, and when it came to confronting the fact that it wasn't working with [the first editor], it was very natural for me to say to myself and to Maura, "Listen, you know, why don't you come in and edit this damn thing . . .?"

It was risky in a way, but it was a risk which, if taken, could provide enormous benefits for both of us. Not only to the product . . .

("What are the benefits for the two of you that you are thinking about?")

. . . further involvement and deeper involvement.

So she helped me edit the [project]. And it worked. It wasn't that easy the first time, just so that this doesn't seem like it was some kind of greeting card. We had horrible days. . . . We had fights. . . . The same kinds of disagreements that two people are liable to have. I said Maura's view of the world—her value system—and mine are congruent, but they're not identical. So, there's the wedge. And the wedge will go in. The same types of disagreements that you would have with any editor, you have, only it's in the context of another relationship, that of husband and wife. And try loading all that other stuff onto a relationship, and you really have a test, a true test of the relationship.

(I asked how the experience had affected the relationship.)

I don't know if there's an old Jewish saying—there probably should be, if there isn't—"Whoever said that you had to be happy." You know, it was an intense experience. . . . It was an exploration, not only of the material at hand, but an exploration of the relationship. . . . [It became] much more of a collaboration—

equal collaboration—in which people who can do what they can do, get a chance to do it.

The boundaries of work genderfication compel men and women to perform according to prescription, without regard to individual needs, values, or capabilities. By working at the boundaries, in order to bring them down, Marty and Maura found freedom: They gave each other the chance to do as individuals what they were each capable of doing.

Facilitate Talk Among Men, Not Man-Talk

A colleague told me the following story:

I remember being a counselor in a dorm and listening to a conversation of a group of residence counselors about sex. They were all guys, and they started talking about their sexual experiences, and each one recounted a full sexual experience, including intercourse, glibly and with ease. And within the following week, each one came to me, individually, and told me he was still a virgin. That's a lot of pressure.

It is a lot of pressure. It comes from striving to meet the idealized excessive demands that I have been discussing, and it influences the behavior of lots of men to engage in man-talk, just as these residence hall counselors were doing.

No matter what their self-doubts may actually be, men often feel compelled to engage in man-talk so as to advertise that they possess the masculine competency cluster requisites. After all, what good is an incompetent man-servant? Women will never give such a man their libidinal bounty.

In order to secure that bounty, all self-doubts must be hidden and a man must boast about the attributes he is supposed to possess. At the same time, other men, through man-talk, are doing the very same boasting. Even if some of the other men's puffery is discounted, an illusion is created, and the world seems filled with competent men competing for women's bounty. As a result, each man's self-doubt grows, feeding the pressure to advertise himself falsely. More man-talk.

Behind their self-assured exteriors, men grow tired and lonely facing the fears and flaws that haunt them. The problem feeds on itself and grows worse because the distortion in communication man-talk creates prevents men from testing their dismal perceptions against reality.

Research evidence tells us that men are less self-disclosing than women. It is no wonder: The ever-increasing burden of self-doubt keeps them silent. They cannot disclose what they suspect about themselves for fear of losing the opportunity to earn a woman's bounty. That's a lot of pressure.

Men can break this cycle of loneliness and striving. By ending their silence about self doubt, men can help themselves debunk the excessive, idealized standards of the male competency cluster.

When, at the end of my interviews, I shared my ideas as well as stories about other men's experiences, including my own, one surprisingly common response was relief and gratitude for the opportunity of conversation with *another man.* Here are some comments:

This was terrific.
Men should do more of it; usually it's something that men don't do.

It's so true. We're trapped.

Everybody's showing—men—that they got the biggest one—whatever, cars, bank accounts, jobs, muscles, you know, friends, travel. It's sick.

I really feel good that we talked. It's nice to hear about other men, and to let it out—about the times you feel like giving it up, you know, you don't have it.

But no one talks. Good old late-night man-to-man, or even man-to-woman, stuff. You don't know how to do it. Someone's got to start.

Yes. That is the problem. Someone must start.

End the Silence

Let us speak about crushing the forces that pressure men into chasing after the forever elusive standards of the male competency cluster, and let us unmask what happens to men who pretend to have attained those standards by *acting* like men rather than by just being themselves, fears and flaws included. Let us reveal what it is like to act powerful but feel vulnerable, and to engage in public boasting but suffer in private. Let us reject rigid prescriptions, traditional and *nouveaux*, about what it means to be a man.

End the silence.

Around the world, men's laws, behaviors, and myths have stereotyped women. They have aided in causing women to be discriminated against, as well as being exploited, and have caused their own self-limiting behavior. Despite the women's movement of recent years, sad remnants of this past remain to burden women:

*   *   *

*Be another pretty face; don't be too assertive, or smart, or any of the things that a man should be. Abide, and your Prince Charming will come, lift you to **his** castle in the clouds, where you will dwell happily forever after.*

And burden men as well:

*Be powerful, decisive, and in all ways Prince Charming—like. Then the maiden will be **yours** and you will dwell happily forever after.*

Let us call attention to these burdens in order to prevent them from becoming tempting beacons, capable of attracting the worst that men and women have to offer one another.

End the silence.

Not all giving is an exchange. Let us speak against the false doctrine of instrumental intimacy which proclaims that men take care of the material and physical world by doing *for, to,* and *in front of* women, while, in exchange, women take care of the emotional world by smoothing its turbulent, jagged edges for men. And when the exchange fails, as it inevitably must, let us boldly expose the disillusionment, blame, rage, and oppression that is expressed in men's complaining, angry shout, "After all I did for her!"

End the silence.

Let us confront work genderfication's self-serving assumption that women are ill-suited for the world of work and that when they enter that "alien" world, they crave, and cannot survive without, a man's *doing for* them.

End the silence.

Man-talk is a way of maintaining the silence while creating the illusion of conversation. A marred inner reality is hidden beneath a guise of perfect manhood. Speakers of man-talk do their best to tell stories that demonstrate they possess Prince Charming attributes. Man-talk distorts reality. Shout it out: Prince Charming had problems too!

End the silence.

        End the silence.

                End the silence.

BIBLIOGRAPHY

Baruch, Grace R., Beiner, Lois B., and Barnett, Rosalind C. Women and gender in research on work and family stress. *American Psychologist*, 42, 4, 130–136 (1987).

Bem, Sandra L. The measurement of psychological androgyny. *Journal of Consulting and Clinical Psychology*, 42, 155–162 (1974).

—————. Sex-role adaptability: One consequence of psychological androgyny. *Journal of Personality and Social Psychology*, 31, 634–643 (1975).

Bernard, Jessie. *American Family Behavior*. New York: Harper, 1952.

—————. The good-provider role: Its rise and fall. *American Psychologist*, 36, 1, 1–12 (1981).

Bettelheim, Bruno. *The Uses of Enchantment*. New York: Vintage, 1977.

Blauner, Robert. *Alienation and Freedom*. Chicago: University of Chicago Press, 1964.

Bly, Robert. *Iron John*. Reading, MA: Addison-Wesley, 1990.

Bossen, Laurel. Women in modernizing societies. *American Ethnologist*, 2, 587–601 (1975).

Brems, Christiana, and Johnson, Mark E. Problem-solving, appraisal and coping style: The influence of sex-role orientation and gender. *Journal of Psychology*, 123, 187–194 (1989).

Brenton, Myron. *The American Male*. New York: Coward-McCann, Inc., 1966.

Briggs, Katherine M. *A Dictionary of British Folk Tales*, 4 vols. Bloomington: Indiana University Press, 1970.

Broverman, Inge K., Vogel, Susan R., Broverman, Donald K., and Clarkson, Frank E. Sex-role stereotypes: A current appraisal. In M.T.S. Mednick, S. S. Tangri, and L. W. Hoffman, eds., *Women and Achievement: Social and Motivational Analyses.* New York: Wiley, 1975.

Brown, D. G. Sex development in a changing culture. *Psychological Bulletin,* 54, 232–242 (1958).

Buss, David M. Human mate selection. *American Scientist,* 73, 47–51 (1985).

Cahn, Dudley D. Relative importance of perceived understanding in developing male-female mate relationships. *Psychological Reports,* 64, 1339–1342 (1989).

Chesler, Phyllis, and Goodman, Emily J. *Women, Money, and Power.* New York: William Morrow, 1976.

Cicone, Michael V., and Ruble, Diane N. Beliefs about males. *Journal of Social Issues,* 34, 5–16 (1978).

Crandall, V. C. Sex differences in the expectancy of intellectual and academic reinforcement. In C. P. Smith, ed., *Achievement Related Motives in Childhood.* New York: Russel Sage, 1969.

David, D., and Brannon, R., eds. *The Forty-Nine Percent Majority: The Male Sex Role.* Reading, MA: Addison-Wesley, 1976.

Deaux, Kay. *The Behavior of Men and Women.* Monterey, CA: Brooks/ Cole, 1976.

Dowling, Colette. *The Cinderella Complex.* New York: Pocket Books, 1982.

Eagly, Alice H. Sex differences in influenceability. *Psychological Bulletin,* 85, 1, 86–116 (1978).

Ellis, Albert. How to live with a neurotic man. *Journal of Rational-Emotive Behavior,* 6, 128–136 (1988).

Fierman, Jaclyn. Do women manage differently? *Fortune,* 115–116 (December 17, 1990).

Frank, Harold H. *Women in the Organization.* Philadelphia: University of Pennsylvania Press, 1977.

Freudenberger, Herbert J. Today's troubled men. *Psychology Today,* 46–47 (1987).

Friedan, Betty. *The Feminine Mystique.* New York: Dell, 1977.

Friedl, Ernestine. *Women and Men: An Anthropologist's View.* New York: Holt, Rinehart & Winston, 1975.

Frieze, Irene B., Parsons, Jacquelynne E., Johnson, Paula B., Ruble, Diane B., and Zellman, Gail L. *Women and Sex Roles: A Social Psychological Perspective.* New York: Norton, 1978.

Frodi, Ann, Macaulay, Jacqueline, and Thorne, Pauline. Are women always less aggressive than men? A review of the experimental literature. *Psychological Bulletin,* 8, 84, 4, 634–660 (1977).

Gilbert, Sandra M., and Gruber, Susan. Sex wars: Not the fun kind. *New York Times Book Review,* 1, 20–22 (December 27, 1987).

Gilmore, David D. *Manhood in the Making: Cultural Concepts of Masculinity.* New Haven, CT: Yale University Press, 1990.

Goodenough, E. W. Interest in persons as an aspect of sex differences in the early years. *Genetic Psychology Monographs,* 55, 287–323 (1957).

Gornick, Vivian, and Moran, Barbara K., eds. *Woman in Sexist Society.* New York: Basic Books, 1971.

Gould, Roger E. Measuring masculinity by the size of a paycheck. In J. E. Pleck and J. Sawyer, eds., *Men and Masculinity.* Englewood Cliffs, NJ: Prentice-Hall, 1974.

Grant, Jan. Woman as managers: What they can offer to organizations. *Organization Dynamics,* 16, 3, 56–63 (1988).

Jourard, S. M., and Richman, P. Disclosure output and input in college students. *Merrill-Palmer Quarterly of Behavioral Development,* 9, 141–148 (1963).

Hantover, Jeffrey P. The Boy Scouts and the validation of masculinity. *Journal of Social Issues,* 34, 184–195 (1978).

Hatfield, J. S., Ferguson, L. R., and Alpert, R. Mother-child interaction and the socialization process. *Journal of Personality and Social Psychology,* 23, 219–233 (1972).

Heilman, Madeline E. Sex bias in work settings: The lack of fit model. In B. Staw and L. Cummings, eds., *Research in Organizational Behavior.* Greenwich, CT: JAI Press, 1983.

———. Sometimes beauty can be beastly. *Sunday New York Times Business Section* (June 22, 1980).

———, and Stopeck, Melanie H. Attractiveness and corporate success: Different causal attributions for males and females. *Journal of Applied Psychology,* 70, 379–388 (1985).

Hennig, Margaret, and Jardim, Anne. *The Managerial Woman*. Garden City, NY: Anchor Press/Doubleday, 1977.

Hoffman, Curt, and Hurst, Nancy. Gender stereotypes: Perception or rationalization. *Journal of Personality and Social Psychology*, 58, 197–208 (1990).

Hoffman, Lois W. Early childhood experiences and woman's achievement motives. In M.T.S. Mednick, S. S. Tangri, and L. W. Hoffman, eds., *Women and Achievement: Social and Motivational Analyses*. New York: Wiley, 1975.

Horner, Matina S. Toward an understanding of achievement-related conflicts in women. *Journal of Social Issues*, 28, 157–175 (1972).

Kanter, Rosabeth M. *Men and Women of the Corporation*. New York: Basic Books, 1977.

Lekarcyzk, D. T., and Hill, K. T. Self-esteem, test anxiety, stress and verbal learning. *Developmental Psychology*, 1, 147–154 (1969).

Letters to the Editor. Management women: Debating the facts of life. *Harvard Business Review*, 182–214 (May/June, 1989).

Lewis, Robert A. Emotional intimacy among men. *Journal of Social Issues*, 34, 108–121 (1978).

Livingstone, D. W., and Luxton, M. Gender consciousness at work: Modification of the male breadwinner norm among steel workers and their spouses. *Canadian Review of Sociology and Anthropology*, 26, 240–275 (1989).

Luebke, Barbara F. Out of focus: Images of women and men in newspaper photographs. *Sex Roles*, 20, 121–133 (1989).

Mabry, Edward A. Some theoretical implications of female and male interaction in unstructured small groups. *Small Group Behavior*, 20, 536–550 (1989).

Maccoby, Eleanor. *The Development of Sex Differences*. Stanford, CA: Stanford University Press, 1966.

————, and Jacklin, Carol N. *The Psychology of Sex Differences*. Stanford, CA: Stanford University Press, 1974.

Mednick, Martha T. S., and Tangri, Sandra S. New social psychological perspectives on women. *Journal of Social Issues*, 28, 1–16 (1972).

Mednick, Martha T. S., Tangri, Sandra S., Hoffman, Lois W., eds. *Women and Achievement: Social and Motivational Analyses*. New York: Wiley, 1975.

Miller, Arthur G., ed. *In the Eye of the Beholder: Contemporary Issues in Stereotyping*. New York: Holt, Rinehart & Winston, 1980.

Monahan, Lynn, Kuhn, Deanna, and Shaver, Phillip. Intrapsychic versus cultural explanations of the "fear of success" motive. *Journal of Personality and Social Psychology*, 29, 60–64 (1974).

O'Leary, Virginia E. Latitudes of masculinity. *Journal of Social Issues*, 34, 17–28 (1978).

————. Some attitudinal barriers to occupational aspirations in women. *Psychological Bulletin*, 81, 809–826 (1974).

————. *Toward Understanding Women*. Monterey, CA: Brooks/Cole, 1977.

Orber, Linda. The analysis of a passive young man involved in fleeting relationships. *Issues in Ego Psychology*, 11, 79–89 (1988).

Pleck, Joseph H. *Working Wives/Working Husbands*. Beverly Hills, CA: Sage, 1985.

————, and Sawyer, Jack. *Men and Masculinity*. Englewood Cliffs, NJ: Prentice-Hall, 1974.

————, and Brannon, Robert, eds. Male roles and the male experience. *Journal of Social Issues*, 34, 1 (1978).

Reskin, Barbara F., ed. *Sex Segregation in the Workplace: Trends, Explanations, Remedies*. Washington, DC: National Academy Press, 1984.

————, and Hartmann, Heidi I. *Women's Work Men's Work. Sex Segregation on the Job*. Washington, DC: National Academy Press, 1986.

Rogers, Susan C. Female forms of power and the myth of male dominance: A model of female/male interaction in peasant society. *American Ethnologist*, 2, 727–756 (1975).

————. Woman's place: A critical review of anthropological theory. *Comparative Studies in Society and History*, 20, 123–162 (1978).

Rose, Suzanna, and Frieze, Irene H. Young singles' scripts for a first date. *Gender and Society*, 3, 258–268 (1989).

Rosener, Judy B. Way women lead. *Harvard Business Review*, 119–125 (November/December 1990).

Rosenzweig, Julie M., and Dailey, Dennis M. Dyadic adjustment/ sexual satisfaction in women and men as a function of psychological sex role self-perception. *Journal of Sex and Marital Therapy,* 15, 42– 56 (1989).

Sanday, Peggy R. *Female Power and Male Dominance: On the Origins of Sexual Inequality.* Cambridge, England: Cambridge University Press, 1988.

————. Toward a theory of the status of women. *American Anthropologist,* 75, 1682–1700 (1973).

Sargent, Alice G. *Beyond Sex Roles.* St. Paul, MN: West Publishing Company, 1977.

Scanzoni, John H. *Sex Roles, Life Styles, and Child Bearing.* New York: Free Press, 1975.

————. *Sexual Bargaining: Power Politics in American Marriage.* Englewood Cliffs, NJ: Prentice-Hall, 1972.

Schaffer, David R., and Wegley, Carol. Success orientation and sex-role congruence as determinants of the attractiveness of competent women. *Journal of Personality,* 42, 586–600 (1974).

Schein, Virginia E. The relationship between sex role stereotypes and requisite management characteristics. *Journal of Applied Psychology,* 57, 95–100 (1973).

Schwartz, Felice N. Management women and the new facts of life. *Harvard Business Review,* 65–76 (January/February 1989).

Small, John E., Rosenwald, Richard J., and Robey, Ames. The wife-beater's wife. *Archives of General Psychiatry* (1964).

Social Behavior. Special issue and perspectives on male role demands, 4, 4 (1989).

Spence, Janet T., and Helmreich, Robert L. *The Psychological Dimensions of Masculinity and Femininity: Their Correlates and Antecedents.* Houston: University of Texas Press, 1978.

————. Who likes competent women: Competence, sex-role congruence of interests, and subjects' attitudes toward women as determinants of interpersonal attraction. *Journal of Applied Social Psychology,* 2, 197–213 (1972).

Taylor, Patricia A., and Glenn, Norral D. The utility of education and attractiveness for females' status attainment through marriage. *American Sociological Review,* 41, 484–498 (1976).

Tiger, Lionel. *Men in Groups.* New York: Random House, 1969.

Udry, J. Richard, and Eckland, Bruce K. Benefits of being attractive: Differential payoffs for men and women. *Psychological Reports,* 54, 47–56 (1984).

Weitzman, Lenore J., Eifler, Deborah, Hokada, Elizabeth, and Ross, Catherine. Sex-role socialization in picture books for pre-school children. *American Journal of Sociology,* 55, 327–332 (1957).

Whiting, Beatrice B. Sex identity conflict and physical violence: A comparative study. *American Anthropologist,* 67, 6, pt. 2, 123–140 (1965).

————, ed. *Six Cultures: Studies of Child Rearing.* New York: Wiley, 1960.

Whiting, John W. M., and Whiting, Beatrice B. Aloofness and intimacy of husbands and wives. *Ethos,* 3, 183–207 (1975).

Zelman, Elizabeth C. Reproduction, ritual and power. *American Ethnologist,* 4, 714–733 (1977).

INDEX

A Note About the Author

HARVEY A. HORNSTEIN has a Ph.D. in social psychology from Teachers College, Columbia University, where he is now Director of the Division of Psychology. He has written several other books, among them *Social Intervention: A Behavioral Science Approach* (Free Press), *Cruelty and Kindness: A New Look at Aggression and Altruism* (Prentice-Hall), and *Managerial Courage: Revitalizing Your Company Without Sacrificing Your Job* (John Wiley).